To Robby +
faithful
friends. You serve us
beyond measure. Dr. Pastor Threatt

Storm Warnings

What stormy conditions lie
before America?

"Watch, Listen, Make Ready,
and Prepare"

Dr. Leon Threatt

Storm Warnings

May be purchased:
www.lulu.com

Copyright @ 2014 by Dr. Leon Threatt

ISBN 978-1-300-55270-3

Special Thanks

To my dear wife Carol, thank you for your love and patience during our thirty-one years of marriage.

To my children and extended family, I say thank you so very much for believing in the grace entrusted to me.

To Christian Faith Assembly, I am eternally grateful for the honor of serving as your pastor for the last twenty-six years.

To all those who have contributed and labored in the publication of this book, I say thank you from the depths of my heart.

Dr. Leon Threatt

Contents

All Scriptural References are King James Version
unless otherwise noted.

"Storm Warnings"

Introduction

Storm clouds loom over the nations, but are we able to discern their counsel? There are ominous, glaring changes and shifts about us, but are we hearing their warnings? Numerous events surrounding the year 2012 and beyond were on the hearts and minds of many. It was believed by some that 2012 was going to be a globally impactful year, and I believe it was that and much more. There was much chatter about what could and might occur during that unusual time in history. There were endless articles written and a few movies produced about the many possibilities believed for 2012 and the years that follows. Much of what was prophesied and feared has not been seen, but I believe far more has occurred than what the natural eye could see.

If the Lord Jesus delays His coming, we will witness just how critically important 2012 was to the direction of America and its impact upon much of the world. In this book we will examine the questions, "What's in store for America during this important junction in time?" and "How are we to prepare our

1

families and communities for a season of unprecedented change and transition?" To those who are devoted Christians you may be asking, "How can I have a meaningful impact upon society for Jesus Christ in such a time as this?"

My earnest desire through these pages is to answer these and many other questions and to encourage your faith in the God who holds the events of man within His grasp. We need to affirm our trust in a faithful Lord at a time when faith and hope of some appear to be waning. We must also attempt to bring some clarity to much of the confusion and uncertainty of the season we are entering. We will examine the scriptures and see what illuminating truths are written about such a time. I propose to address a number of important questions including:

- What is God speaking to His Body about such a time?
- Can we know some of what is to come?
- Has and is God speaking to the hearts of His people about this approaching season and the coming events?
- What is the Holy Spirit saying?

2

- What are we appointed and commissioned to do in this hour?
- How do we who are born of the Holy Spirit communicate faith, hope and rest to a fearful and hopeless generation?

Jesus alone is the answer to man's deepest and most urgent questions. Church, we have a responsibility as the Body of Christ to bring the message of hope and redemption to our generation. We are charged to bring the truth with clarity and relevance so that others can make an informed decision to live or not to live for Christ Jesus. We must know the season and hour in which we live. We have to recognize the approaching times in order to answer and refute many of the concerns and uncertainties that face this generation. We need true discernment like never before.

<u>Know and recognize the signs that mark this generation.</u>

> *"He answered and said to them, 'When it is evening you say, It will be fair weather, for the sky is red; and in the morning, It will be foul weather today, for the sky is red and threatening. Hypocrites! You know how to discern the face of*

the sky, but you cannot discern the signs of the times'" (Matthew 16:2,3) (NKJV).

We must not be like the generation that Jesus was addressing. They were not able to recognize their privileged hour. They would have been graced to see, touch and hear the Living Savior of the world; but, they were not discerning and attentive enough to recognize Him.

The Church must be as discerning as the sons of Issachar. Issachar was one of the tribes of Israel that joined young King David while he was in the wilderness fleeing from King Saul. The sons of Issachar were men who had understanding of the times and seasons and had clarity of what Israel should do.

> *"...sons of Issachar who had understanding (knowledge, meaning, wisdom) of the times (season), to know what Israel ought to do..."* (First Chronicles 12:32) (NKJV).

The Lord still speaks to His servants the prophets. The Lord wills to reveal His intentions and many of the pending events before they occur. He does so because He loves His creation and desires to care and protect those who belong to Him.

"Surely the Lord God will do nothing, but He revealeth His secret unto His servants the prophets" (Amos 3:7).

The Body of Christ must hear from the Lord! We must hear from the Lord what is soon to occur and intercede for grace and mercy on the behalf of the righteous and the unrighteous of humanity.

"...And the Lord said, Shall I hide from Abraham that thing which I do...but Abraham stood yet before the Lord. And Abraham drew near, and said, Wilt thou also destroy the righteous with the wicked?..." (Genesis 18:16-33).

Abraham interceded for the safety of the righteous that was in Sodom and Gomorrah. The Lord Jesus has come to give life, not to take life!

The Holy Spirit alone reveals the deep things of God unto His Body.

"...But God hath revealed them unto us by His Spirit: for the Spirit searcheth all things, yea, the deep things of God..." (First Corinthians 2:6-16); *"My sheep hear my voice, and I know them, and they follow me"* (St. John 10:27).

We can and will know the times, seasons and signs by the witness of the Holy Spirit. He will unveil and reveal the deep mysteries of God to His watchful sons and daughters, and obedient servants.

We who are in Christ Jesus must know and recognize the signs of the times like never before. We must be discerning and hearing the voice of the Holy Spirit in order to wisely communicate His heart and mind to this generation. Out of His great love for creation He alerts and forewarns a people of any pending judgments. He sends warning signs and witnesses in an earnest attempt to save and spare the innocent and righteous from sure destruction. Just as meteorologist study the science of the atmosphere in order to accurately forecast the weather, so there must be a people who search the heart and mind of God in order to accurately communicate the conditions that are soon to come upon us.

There is a storm approaching unlike anything we have ever seen. Storms mark the changing of times and seasons. As a three and one-half year drought was ending for Elijah and King Ahab, so is there a changing season upon the nations of the earth. King Ahab and Jezebel, his wife, had lead Israel into idolatry and rebellion, but their evil days of rule was being numbered.

> *"Then Elijah said to Ahab, 'Go up, eat and drink; for there is the sound of abundance of rain.' So Ahab went up to eat and drink. And Elijah went up to the top of Carmel; then he bowed down on the ground, and put his face between his knees, and said to his servant, 'Go up now, look toward the sea.' So he went up and looked, and said, 'There is nothing.' And seven times he said, 'Go again.' Then it came to pass the seventh time, that he said, 'There is a cloud, as small as a man's hand, rising out of the sea!' So he said, 'Go up, say to Ahab, Prepare your chariot, and go down before the rain stops you.' Now it happened in the meantime that the sky became black with clouds and wind, and there was a heavy rain. So Ahab rode away and went to Jezreel"* (First Kings 18:41-45) (NKJV).

This book is an earnest attempt to examine and communicate the conditions and circumstances that will affirm that a horrific global storm is approaching. The warnings, the notices, and the alarms are being sounded to alert all of the advancement of a storm that will be unlike anything we have ever witnessed before. Elijah instructs King Ahab to "Prepare." We too must prepare and make ready; for the "Storm Warnings" are being declared!

Chapter One

WHAT DOES THE HOLY SCRIPTURES SAY ABOUT SUCH A TIME?

"For God did not appoint us to wrath, but to obtain salvation through our Lord Jesus Christ,"
(First Thessalonians 5:9) (NKJV)

Let's examine what the Holy Scriptures say about such a time as this. It is written in the Word that in the last days difficult and perilous times shall come.

> *"But know this, that in the last days perilous times will come"* (Second Timothy 3:1) (NKJV).

In Greek, the word "perilous" means difficult, dangerous and furious times. The last days are from the ascension of Jesus until this very day. The Apostle Paul goes on in this letter to communicate a description of what those last days would look like.

> *"For men will be lovers of themselves, lovers of money, boasters, proud, blasphemers, disobedient*

9

to parents, unthankful, unholy, unloving, unforgiving, slanderers, without self-control, brutal, despisers of good, traitors, headstrong, haughty, lovers of pleasure rather than lovers of God, having a form of godliness but denying its power. And from such people turn away!" (Second Timothy 3:2-5) (NKJV)

As I read these verses it is so very clear to me that our present generation seems to fit this description of the last days better than any reported generation before it.

The Apostle Paul also communicates to the church in Thessalonica that the day of Christ is at hand, but would not fully manifest except there come a falling away first.

"Let no one deceive or beguile you in any way, for that day will not come except the apostasy comes first (unless the predicted great falling away of those who have professed to be Christians has come), and the man of lawlessness (sin) is revealed, who is the son of doom (of perdition)" (Second Thessalonians 2:3) (Amplified).

The words "falling away" are from the Greek "Apostasia" which means apostasy, defection from truth or to forsake. This season of apostasy will precede an aggressive and climactic revolt against the known will of God. It will prepare the way for the appearance of the man of sin. We are witnessing this to some degree even today. Entire church denominations are forsaking the written Word of God and following human fables. Some of these same denominations are ordaining homosexuals into the ministry and embracing same sex marriages.

We read similar words of apostasy from the Apostle Paul to Timothy in his first letter.

> *"Now the Spirit speaketh expressly, that in the latter times some shall depart from the faith, giving heed to seducing spirits, and doctrines of devils; speaking lies in hypocrisy..."* (First Timothy 4:1,2).

Departing from the faith is the departing from the truth of God's Word. Many of those who depart will still congregate, but will be listening to seducing spirits and doctrines of devils. I thought of those professing Christians who have embraced Chrislam. This is without question doctrines of devils. What is Chrislam? It is the godless attempt to combine

Christianity and Islam. How can two walk together without being in agreement? They cannot!

The day of the Lord shall come as a thief.

> *"But concerning the times and the seasons, brethren, you have no need that I should write to you. For you yourselves know perfectly that the day of the Lord so comes as a thief in the night. For when they say, 'Peace and safety!' then sudden destruction comes upon them, as labor pains upon a pregnant woman. And they shall not escape. But you, brethren, are not in darkness, so that this Day should overtake you as a thief. You are all sons of light and sons of the day. We are not of the night nor of darkness. Therefore let us not sleep, as others do, but let us watch and be sober"* (First Thessalonians 5:1-6) (NKJV).

There is so much insight and wisdom from these verses. The Apostle is bringing insight to the time of the "coming of the Lord." The day will happen suddenly and quickly and we should prepare and make ready. This entire chapter is filled with insight and encouragement pertaining to the hour that we currently live in. However, verse nine warrants our watchful attention. It reads:

"For God did not appoint us to wrath, but to obtain salvation through our Lord Jesus Christ," (5:9).

God has not appointed the Church to experience His wrath. The whole earth will experience the wrath of God during the tribulation period. Therefore, we must remain in a constant state of readiness. We who are in Christ should not be surprised and taken off guard by the coming of the Lord, nor by any events that may precede His coming. We should not be found asleep as others, but watching and living sober lives. After the coming of the Lord, what we call the rapture or the catching away of the Body of Christ, the earth will be plunged into seven years of the wrath of God.

The time that we are living in now is described in Luke 17:26,27:

"And as it was in the days of Noah, so it will be also in the days of the Son of Man: They ate, they drank, they married wives, they were given in marriage, until the day that Noah entered the ark, and the flood came and destroyed them all" (NKJV).

In Noah's day according to Genesis 6:5:

> *"...God saw that the wickedness of man was great in the earth, and that every imagination of the thoughts of his heart was only evil [bad, wrong, wretchedness, harm] continually."*

Noah's generation rejected the warning of pending judgment and suffered accordingly.

We also read that as it was in the days of Lot so it will be in the days of the coming of the Lord.

> *"...They ate, they drank, they bought, they sold, they planted, they built; but on the day that Lot went out of Sodom it rained fire and brimstone from heaven and destroyed them all..."* (Luke 17:28-30) (NKJV).

God brought judgment because their sin was "very grievous."

> *"...the cry of Sodom and Gomorrah is great, and because their sin is very grievous"* (Genesis 18:20); *"And they called unto Lot, and said unto him...bring them out unto us, that we may know them [have homosexual relations]"* (Genesis 19:5).

The spirit of Sodom is a vile, violent, militant spirit. It has no regard for neither divine nor the sacred things of God. These wicked men attempted to sexually violate angels. Note that the removal of Lot and his family is a type of the "rapture." After Lot's departure, judgment was brought upon the two cities. After the rapture of the Church, judgment will be released upon all of the earth. Humanity will face unimaginable wrath. Those of Sodom and Gomorrah also rejected the words of Lot. Again, look at Luke 17:30:

> *"Even thus shall it be in the day when the Son of man is revealed."*

Wow, what a statement! According to the verse, the day when the Son of man Jesus the Anointed King is revealed will be very much as it was in the days of Noah and Lot. The revealing of the Son of man is the rapture of the Church and the physical return of Jesus on the Mount of Olives. They are called the "return of Christ." Two parts are separated by seven years of the wrath of God upon the earth.

The scriptures also communicate a number of signs describing the return of Christ. Many of those signs are recorded in Matthew 24:3-51:

> *"...what shall be the sign of thy coming, and of the end of the world [age]?...many shall come in my name, saying, I am Christ; and shall deceive*

> *many...wars and rumors of wars...nation shall rise against nation, and kingdom against kingdom: and there shall be famines [hunger], and pestilences [pledges, disease], and earthquakes, in divers places..."*

The referenced verses also speak of persecution for the name of Christ Jesus and an increase of offense, betrayal, and hatred.

> *"And many false prophets shall rise, and shall deceive many. And because iniquity [lawlessness, wickedness] shall abound [increase and multiply], the love [agape God's love] of many shall wax cold [chill]...this gospel of the Kingdom shall be preached in all the world for a witness unto all nations; and then shall the end come"* (Matthew 24:11,12,14).

In verse 32, the parable of the fig tree tells us that we would know that summer is nigh. The restoration of the nation of Israel in 1948 is believed to be fulfilled in this verse. In verse 34, we read that this generation would not pass till all these things are fulfilled.

I believe that the coming of the Lord is sooner than any might think!

Wisdom to Remember: The appearing of the Lord Jesus Christ will come as a thief in the night, and only the upright and the ready will rejoice on that day!

Chapter Two

WHAT ARE WE HEARING AND DISCERNING?

"He who testifies to these things says, 'Surely I am coming quickly.' Amen. Even so, come, Lord Jesus! The grace of our Lord Jesus Christ be with you all. Amen." (Revelation 22:20,21) (NKJV)

I truly believe that God wants us to hear and understand the times in which we presently live. During a moment of prayer and meditation in October 2011 I sought the Lord's wisdom about this subject and I believe I heard a number of revealing things from Him. I asked the Lord very pointed questions about the year 2012 and the seasons beyond, and the Holy Spirit responded. He spoke to my heart and I heard it just as I have written it here:

"Prepare My people for My coming. My coming is near. Don't be afraid to declare 'Repent for the King is at hand.' I delay but for a moment out of mercy for the lost. Cry out to them for the judgment is before those who refuse to repent and turn to the Living God.

Spare not to declare the Word, the King is at Hand. I am stirring and shaking nations with My great love for all. I'm shaking those things that are not eternal and must fall from them. I shake those things out of My great love."

The very last recorded words of Jesus are found in Revelation 22:20, '...*Surely I am coming quickly*' (NKJV). The Lord continued to speak to my heart:

"I continue to call My Church to holiness, purity, and righteousness. Live set apart unto Me! Your many sins have come up before Me. Sin is judged. Be the witness that I have appointed you to be. I have given you My Spirit, Word, and My Name. Go forward with full authority to do My will. The nations await your obedience to Me. Refuse to fear. Be bold, strong and courageous. My coming is near!"

In this time of prayer and intercession I heard and saw many things. I began to seek the Lord for clarity and insight on what I was hearing and seeing including:

What about Israel?
"Pray for My chosen people. Cry for their safety. My work for them is not complete. I will finish in

them what I have begun. Cry out for My grace and glory to manifest in My Land of Promise."

How should we address and confront Islam?

"Don't be afraid of their lies. I am drawing many out of the lie into the truth. Many are the seed of Abraham and I love them. You must love them also. Cry out for their souls. I find no pleasure in their eternal death."

How about America?

"The growing sins of America are great in My sight. You have lived as hypocrites. You demand from others what you refused to live. Continued judgment is upon you. I have not judged you, your many sins are judged. I have been merciful and patient with you, longing for your repentance. But you have refused My invitation to repent."

What will our judgment look like?

"Much of it is what you have never witnessed before. The measure of your gross sins will be the measure of your judgment. You once were a light to the nations, but you have walked away from the source of your light. The abundance of your many sins is spilling out and overflowing. Those things done in secret are spilling out and are seen by others. The secrets of the hearts are coming to light. Your unrighteous leaders will have to give account. Their judgment shall be greater for they have led many astray."

How about Your Church?

"I do have many who have remained upright, repentant and faithful. Be strong and courageous until the end. Don't give up or give in. My hour is near. Your day of reward is soon to come. You are My chosen people, refuse to compromise. I hate when you do that. Live fully unto Me. Encourage one another for the hope that's in you. Live and love as one church. Proclaim My Word without compromise. Believe Me for miracles."

What about Church leaders?

"I will deal with them. You need not concern yourself with such. I raise up one and I sit down another. You fully follow My Word and leave judgment to Me. Guard your hearts and your tongues."

What is important for us in 2012 and beyond?

"There will be an increase of spiritual activities. Darkness knows that their hour of judgment is near. There will also be a recognizable increase of the operation of My Spirit. I'm putting a demand on the fruit of the spirit. I will also move mightily in the gifts of My Spirit. The nations will be watching America closely in 2012. It will be seen by the nations. The true intent and hearts of global leaders will be exposed and made clear. Your money will not be able to support you. Its weakness will be exposed. For many, great fear will fill their hearts. Birth pains, contractions will begin and intensify. The nations will experience the birthing of My will, plans, and purposes. I am working out all matters according to My eternal will. Some are crying out 'peace, peace.' They will say, 'things are as they have always been.' Don't listen to their lies. I have not sent them. They are speaking out of their own hearts. In 2012, the judgment of sin will increase. The quick and swift judgment shall be seen. Know the times that you are living in. The gospel shall bring hope, life and peace to nations like they have only dreamed of. Send forth the gospel to the four corners of the world. The gospel is man's only hope. Invest deeply into it. It alone will produce the hope humanity longs for."

I have also heard and sensed that this is a prophetic season. We are prophetic people and are sent forth for such a time as this! Proclaim God's will into a matter. Refuse to fear what you see and hear. Exercise faith in Him. He will never leave nor forsake His Church. Rest in His Word and in His promises. Do the work of the Evangelist. Seek men to be reconciled to God! Commit and live a set apart life. Give yourself to prayer, fasting, reading, and studying the Word. Seek His face with your whole heart. The year 2012, for some of the people of God, was the beginning of a season of miraculous manifestations in order to fulfill His Word and work in the earth.

Wisdom to Remember: God warns and admonishes people and nations out of His great love for them, and is not willing that any would perish, but that all would come to repentance.

Chapter Three

WHAT ARE OTHERS SAYING ABOUT THIS SEASON AND BEYOND?

"He who has an ear, let him hear what the Spirit says to the churches. To him who overcomes I will give to eat from the tree of life, which is in the midst of the Paradise of God."
(Revelation 2:7) (NKJV)

There are a lot of fear producing discussions coming from many sources. We must listen with our hearts being sensitive to the Holy Spirit. Some had said that 21 December 2012 was going to be the day when the planets would all uniquely align themselves which would produce an atmospheric change. Some economists had predicted the fall of the American dollar, which would have caused major economic fallout. They said that the economic fall would have global implications. There are endless streams of prophecies and declarations coming from all directions both within and outside of the Church. We must hear what the Lord says to the seven churches of Asia Minor; recorded in Revelation 2:7 Jesus said to all seven churches:

> *"He who has an ear, let him hear what the Spirit says to the churches..."* (NKJV).

The Holy Spirit is the only Person in the earth that knows everything about the times and seasons we are in and soon to enter. We must seek to hear from Him. We too must remain watchful and attentive to what Jesus Christ is speaking to His church and to humanity at large.

Kenneth Copeland

At the Victory Campaign on November 10, 2011 in Washington, DC, Mr. Copeland asked the Lord the following questions:

- What about 2012?
- What does it hold?
- What's in store for the nations?
- What's in store for Israel and what's in store for the Church?

"'Oh yes! 2012 is a time of miracles. Miracles that seemed as if they would not come but they're here. There is an atmosphere conducive to miracles that's been growing and growing and will manifest greatly in the first quarter of 2012 and continue throughout the year and on into 2013. I've been looking forward to 2012,' saith The LORD. 'I know how it's going to turn out. I've already dealt with it in My WORD. Your future is looking better all the time. But of course you'll need to look at it through My eyes,' saith the Spirit of grace. So as I said before, rejoice, for your time has come."[1]

Pastor Christopher Cookhorne

"For 2012 His people must be prepared. It will be a time of unusual miracles for the saints to receive, even though warfare will intensify."[2]

Dr. Bill Hamon

"God is speaking to me that 2012 will be a year of Possessing for Progress and Prosperity. We have come through a time of testing, and now it is time for us to possess the resources and press on to see the Third and Final Reformation progressing in the earth."[3]

Kim Clement

"The Spirit of the Lord came upon me again. He said, 'I'm speaking about 2012 and 2013.' He spoke to me about this. He said, '2012 to 2013 – for a seven-year period – it's going to go up. Everything's going to move upward. I'm going to bring about a move of My Spirit, a shaking, for My goodness will be seen by the people. For a seven-year period, you're going to have exactly the opposite to what you've been experiencing now.' Now God says, and says to you, the people of God, 'All I need for you to do is to believe it and to pray it, for I will watch over My revelation. I will watch over My Word and I will perform it,' says the Lord. 'But only those that will speak it shall receive it first.'"4

Dr. Pat Robertson

"Internal stress in America will tear it apart. A house divided cannot stand. How can you be content when millions are going to hell? There is an urgent call for prayer. Loose the bounds of wickedness. The future of the world is at stake. A time of Maximum stress. Disintegrate. Stress beyond any before. Caused by an economic collapse. It's not God's judgment, but your own choosing. The next President will grip the controls like an airplane pilot does as a plane is heading for a crash. Expect chaos. There are great things in the Lord. The Spirit of God will do great things."5

As I have penned these words of those who communicated a word of encouragement and prophecy I have sincerely attempted to document each of them accurately. You may go to their websites and read their words in its entirety.

You may notice that much of what has been communicated in this chapter has been centered on the year 2012. There are many reasons why that is the case, one of which is, 2012 was a critically important year in the spirit realm. I believe a spiritual shift took place that year. The nations came to a critical crossroad. It was a time when new directions were offered and a fresh start was granted to nations and to individuals. It was so evident that America was granted a renewed opportunity to return to the God of the Bible. Our nation was given place before a Holy God to repent of its rebellion, lawlessness, corruption, and wickedness. As we have pressed beyond that famed year it is evident to me and to others that America has rejected the merciful hand of Almighty God and has plunged ever deeper into debauchery. In 2012, the nation elected and re-elected vile godless leaders. In 2012, our courts continued to legislate the continuous murder of the unborn. From 2012 on, our nation has continued to entertain the abominable spirit of Sodom. Much of the church community and its leadership have consistently moved away from sound biblical teaching. Many no longer affirm the inerrancy of Holy Scripture. Throughout human history our merciful God has offered to nations place and grace to repent and return to Him. We read such in the prayer request of King Solomon and God's response to King Solomon. It is recorded in Second Chronicles 7:14:

> *"If my people, which are called by my name, shall humble themselves, and pray, and seek my face, and turn from their wicked ways; then will I hear from heaven, and will forgive their sin, and will heal their land."*

It is my contention that in 2012 America was granted a similar opportunity, but sadly to say I don't believe we humbled ourselves, prayed, sought His face, nor did America turn from its wicked ways. Therefore, it is my belief that 2012 was the beginning of the end for this nation and for much of the world.

Wisdom to Remember: God alone has infinite knowledge and understanding of the times and seasons in which we live, yet

He does reveal what He chooses to those who are willing to listen.

Chapter Four

BELIEVING GOD IN THIS SEASON AND BEYOND

"Jesus said to him, 'If you can believe, all things are possible to him who believes.'" (Mark 9:23) (NKJV)

What should we believe God for during this unusual season? There certainly are an endless list of needs and concerns facing our nation and communities. Here are several critically important things that I am trusting, seeking and believing God for in the days and years to come.

<u>Limitless Living</u>. I am seeking the heart of God for limitless living, where all things are possible for those who believe would fully manifest. Man's greatest achievement is to believe God according to His Word. We will consistently live at the point of our true faith in God.

> *"Jesus said...'If you can believe, all things are possible to him who believes'"* (Mark 9:23) (NKJV).

A Sustained Move of His Spirit. May we witness in this season a sustained move of His Spirit and glory in the lives of those who are a part of the Body of Christ. I so long to see a sustained move of the Holy Spirit and the manifestations of the glory and wonder of the Lord Jesus Christ in the personal lives, families and homes of the people of God. Now is the time for the Holy Spirit to have free access to fully work the living Word into our daily lives.

Open Doors for the Gospel of Jesus Christ. This is the day for the Body of Christ to boldly and unashamedly proclaim the good news of Jesus Christ with all diligence. The Gospel of Jesus Christ is lost humanity's greatest and most urgent need. The Apostle Paul communicates it so profoundly.

> *"For I am not ashamed of the gospel of Christ: for it is the power of God unto salvation to everyone that believeth; to the Jew first, and also to the Greek. For therein is the righteousness of God revealed from faith to faith: as it is written, the just shall live by faith"* (Romans 1:16,17).

By faith, may the years that follow 2012 be a season that countless souls are won to the Kingdom of Jesus Christ. Now is the day that we all would faithfully live and serve the Lord Jesus Christ with the heart of the evangelist.

Men of God. My faith is in the God that changes not. Our families, communities and churches suffer for a lack of faithfulness among men. My heart's desire is to see men who are born of God take their place at the helms and heads of their families. I'm believing God that men of faith would recognize, understand and embrace their divinely given roles as heads of households. There are far too many mothers, sisters and daughters leading their homes without the leadership of a man of God. Brothers, it is time to return to our homes. It's now in this season that men of courage must take the moral leadership within their communities. And yes, it is high time for faithful, upright and biblically sound men to return to their place in the church. Most of the service in the local church is conducted by women. It is a wonderful thing to witness as our sisters serve so faithfully, but let it not be because there are so few men to step up and do it.

Effective Ministry Among Children and Youth. Let us believe the Lord for increased effectiveness in our service and ministry among children and youth. The elevation of children and youth ministry will continue to be a critically important part in the work of the Kingdom. Our children and youth are believed to be the most vulnerable and yet most valuable asset in society. Both groups are a serious concern upon my heart and I believe they are also a pressing priority upon the heart of our heavenly Father. Many have said that in these last hours before the coming of our King, that our youth and children would be mightily used by God. Let it be so Lord Jesus!

The Restoration of the Tithe and Offerings. It is extremely important to the work of the Kingdom, and to my own heart, to witness the returning of the tithes and offerings to the household of faith. We all know that the "tithe" is ten percent of the first and best of all our income. It was and is my prayer and desire to witness the year 2012 and beyond be the beginning of a time and season for the release and restoration of the tithes and offerings to the church of the Lord Jesus Christ. One of the most profound truths pertaining to tithing for the present church age is found in Hebrews 7:8:

> *"And here men that die receive tithes; but there he receiveth them, of whom it is witnessed that he liveth."*

Wow! Our tithes is a testimony that we believe that Jesus Christ is alive as our High Priest and there in heaven receiving our tithes. Let me say that again, "Tithing among other things is a testimony of our faith in God that we believe that Jesus Christ yet lives and receives our tithes there in heaven." Awesome!

Debt Free Living. I believe that the Lord is doing a wonderful and marvelous thing in these last days. I discern by the Spirit that we have entered into a season that will usher in a divine supernatural supply. This divine supply is to accomplish a number of things. It is to move His people out of insufficiency into debt free living. As the nation of Israel exited Egypt with no debt and loaded up with provisions for service and worship, so it is to be for His people of today. We must believe God for the provisions, for He alone is the source. By faith we must believe that His church has entered a time and season of miraculous financial breakthroughs and supernatural debt cancellations. With the divine hand of the Lord working in our personal and church finances we must purpose to eliminate all debt from our lives. I am seeing a season of an abundance of provision to support the Gospel of Jesus Christ like we have never seen before. I am hearing the sound of rain, but it is the sound of an abundant supernatural supply. It is going to be so very important that the Body of Christ not hold onto the increase given by God, but release it for the gospel's sake.

Ready and Watchful Living. Lastly, I'm believing God for His Body the Church, to live a ready, watchful and prepared lifestyle. By the grace of the Living God may those in the family of Jesus Christ prepare their hearts and lives for what lay in the days and years to come. By the work of the Holy Spirit and the operation of the Word we must prepare our families, homes, communities, and churches for all God has in store; and may He continue to have mercy and grace on our souls.

Wisdom to Remember: There are absolutely no limitations with God; only limitations of faith in God!

Chapter Five

WISDOM FOR READINESS!
WHAT MUST WE DO AS WE ENTER AND
PROGRESS THROUGH THIS SEASON?

*"For you died, and your life is hidden
with Christ in God. When Christ who is
our life appears, then you also will
appear with Him in glory."*
(Colossians 3:3,4) (NKJV)

"Prepare" is the optimum word! We must commit to an urgent readiness—spiritually, emotionally, mentally, psychologically, physically, financially, and ministerial (servant hood). The book of Jeremiah gives a unique challenge to us all.

> *"If thou hast run with the footmen, and they have wearied thee, then how canst thou contend with horses?..."* (Jeremiah 12:5).

Those who are unprepared are quickly overwhelmed in the time of difficulty and trial. As I communicate this I am fully aware that some Christians have a completely different view on preparation. They may be comfortable with the spiritual and emotional preparation, but fully disagree with some of the practical preparations shared in this book. On that note I leave the level and degree of preparation to each and every family and individual. There are some Believers that may say it is a lack of faith and trust in God's divine care to store food and supplies. Others may even say for a church or Believers to seek training in handgun safety and self-defense is sin and unbelief. Again, I communicate to each of you that each person, family, church, and community must find that place that they believe is God's leading for them. I do admit that much of my approach for readiness and preparation comes from my own life experiences. Being a former Marine and former Law Enforcement Officer has availed me a view of life that most do not have; not necessarily an advantage, but a unique perspective on life and personal safety.

Storms and natural disasters can be very challenging for a city and state. Watching the devastating images of New Orleans, Louisiana caused by Hurricane Katrina was heart breaking. Many of us were moved to tears by the countless news reports, but those who lived through it have a far more vivid and painful perspective. I'm sure most, if not all, would say a greater degree of preparation was desperately needed. I am also sure all would have preferred to have been elsewhere. How could the people, city and state have better prepared themselves for such devastation? That question will continue to be examined for many years to come. Many who lived in the Charlotte, North Carolina area may recall the destruction caused by Hurricane Hugo on September 22, 1989. I was serving as a Charlotte Police Officer at the time and witnessed much of the pains and destruction first hand. I was working during that night just a block away from I-85 and East Sugar Creek Road. The power and force of the winds were unlike anything I had ever seen. I witnessed two hundred year old oak trees tumble with little resistance. Seasoned pines snapped like twigs. There were only a few deaths caused by the storm, but the county suffered millions of dollars in property damage. How does a city handle and face such storms? How and what can a family do to survive and even thrive during such a time? I believe only through watchful, careful, and prayerful preparation can we begin to minimize the loss of life and property destruction.

America, I believe there is a storm approaching this nation like we have never witnessed before. This storm will reach from east coast to west coast and from our northern boarders to our southern boundaries. This storm of difficulty will greatly disrupt our normal way of life beyond our wildest imagination. I believe this storm will shake every institution in this country. It will not be business as usual! Some may ask, where are you getting your information? For the last few years I have consistently heard in my spirit from the Lord, "Prepare." As time has passed the warning cry has gotten louder and clearer. I am hearing from the Spirit of the Lord, "Prepare for the storm. Clouds are approaching!" I believe we must prepare our lives, families, communities, and churches with a great sense of urgency. The quality of our preparation will determine the quality of our safety. How do we prepare for such a storm? Here are a number of guidelines and recommendations that I have put forth for my home and my church. I trust they will give some direction to you as well.

Please know that our preparation should not be done with a sigh of hopelessness, but in full faith and confidence in the Lord who is more than sufficient to care for His own. I do believe there is still hope for America, but it will demand genuine repentance and a returning to the one true God who made it great. At the present course of direction America is heading into a storm of difficulty unlike anything we have ever witnessed or could imagine. Therefore, Prepare!

<u>Live a prayerful and fasted life</u>. I have a friend who is a pastor and he has posted at the front of his church pulpit the words, "Much prayer, much power; Little prayer, little power; No prayer, no power." I so agree with those words. Some would ask, "Why should we have to pray, God knows what we have need of?" That's true, He does; but He asks that we come to Him and seek His face. We must come to Him in faith and confidence in the eternal reality of who He is. I believe God asks of us to participate in His process of intervention here in the earth. Prayer is a type of invitation to God for His presence and assistance into the affairs of humanity. Jesus said to His disciples in Luke 18:1:

"…men ought always to pray, and not to faint."

Prayer is not work. It is fellowship and cooperation with the plans and will of God. Prayer is communion with God about the affairs of His world and our lives.

Prayer is receiving instructions and communicating our hearts to the King and Commanding Chief of the universe. What an honor! As a former Marine I understand the value of a time to give attention to orders and reporting to headquarters pertinent information. The Lord has designed His system and plan of involvement into the issues that face His creation and prayer is central to His plan. What an awesome opportunity for humanity to have access to the Creator of heaven and earth through prayer. He invites us into His work here in the earth, and prayer is a necessary part of that process.

The fasted life appears to be a forgotten discipline for much of the church of today. I find it interesting that so few followers of Jesus Christ consistently fast. We purpose at Christian Faith Assembly where I serve, to set aside seasons of prayer and fasting throughout the year. Yet, it comes to my attention that many throughout the Body of Christ still struggle with this simple but vital discipline called fasting. I believe partly because we live in a time when self-indulgence is so available. There is food at every corner. The average American home wastes more food than it eats. With so much food in our faces every day, pushing the plate away becomes a real battle for many. Fasting is very important to personal growth and maturity in our walk of faith in Christ. We must be able to mortify the deeds of the flesh and fasting is an essential part in that process. We have to be able to say no to the many lusts and appetites that pull at our hearts and minds each day. I have found that a consistent life of fasting is vital to this disciplined life in Christ. Fasting is not intended to move God; it moves us to a place to hear and obey God.

I have always been uncomfortable with the idea of trying to do anything that would attempt to move God. Our Father is perfectly positioned and does not need to move. In the finished work of Jesus Christ we have all things that pertain to life and godliness. So why is fasting so important? Fasting is one of the daily disciplines that are needed to help us to train our inner man to remain faithful to what we are charged to do. Fasting buffets the body and soul to stand firm in the path of life and obedience. We train our flesh and soul to consistently walk according to God's Word. We bring ourselves under control and present our bodies a living sacrifice unto God, which is our reasonable service (Romans 12:1). The Word of the Lord communicates the reason and kind of fast that He is asking of us. According to Isaiah 58:6:

"Is not this the fast that I have chosen? To loose the bands of wickedness, to undo the heavy burdens, and to let the oppressed go free, and that ye break every yoke?"

Did you get that last statement? To break every yoke! Fasting helps break the yokes of bondage, addiction, habits, and much more. As a young Christian I had a number of issues; okay, they were sins and strongholds. I was taught by my mentors and by the Word that fasting was necessary to break those yokes. It has consistently worked for me. I believe whatever vice, habit, addiction or stronghold that may have gripped your soul, can be broken through God's Word, His Spirit and a consistent life of fasting. Deliverance does not come by fasting, but it helps break the grip and hold. We are delivered and redeemed by the Blood of the Lord Jesus Christ. He alone sets the captives free. Fasting helps break and sustain the emotional and physical hold those things may have had. An essential part of preparation for the events that are forthcoming demands a fasted life. Learning to discipline the body and flesh today will help sustain the victory in the time of battle tomorrow.

Give yourselves to the Word of God. We must give ourselves to reading, studying, meditating, and obeying the written logos word.

> *"All scripture is given by inspiration of God, and is profitable for doctrine, for reproof, for correction, for instruction in righteousness: That the man of God may be perfect, thoroughly furnished unto all good works"* (Second Timothy 3:16,17).

We must go deeper into the scriptures than we have gone before. Deeper in the sense of a greater commitment, a greater devotion and a greater resolve to obey God's Word. In verse 17, the Word causes the man and woman of God to be perfect and mature. It will be this kind of grounded Christian character that we must exercise in the days and hours to come. There must also be a firm assurance and confidence in the reliability and inerrancy of the scriptures. The enemy will work endlessly to bring doubt and question to the written Word of God, just as he did against Eve.

"...hath God said...?" (Genesis 3:1).

It will be the scriptures that we will need to defeat him as Jesus did.

"...It is written..." (Matthew 4:4).

It will be the living, active, eternal Word of God that will produce wisdom, strength and victory in our everyday lives.

Proclaim the Gospel of Jesus Christ with all diligence and make disciples. There is an urgency in the proclamation of the good news of Jesus Christ! The gospel is the power of God unto salvation according to Romans 1:16. We are to seek for creative and innovative ways to share Christ Jesus with all those we can. There must be a concerted effort from the Body of Christ to proclaim the Gospel with sincere love, true compassion and Biblical accuracy. Part of the message that must be preached and proclaimed is "repent for the King is at hand!" With our proclamation there must come a genuine commitment to God's Word for making disciples of all nations and people. It will not be enough to teach and preach the truth of God; we must also seek to make faithful followers of Jesus Christ. Disciples! Amen!

Live in and by the King and His Kingdom. This is the hour and season for the full and undeniable manifestations of the Kingdom of God. We must live a consistent life of faith and obedience to His Word without compromise. The Kingdom functions and operates by the spoken Word. Effective and accurate speech will help us move into the work of the Kingdom. We must speak God's Word, which is the constitution of God's eternal Kingdom. Just as Jesus and John the Baptist proclaimed the Kingdom in their ministry, so we too must declare the Kingdom of God is upon us.

> *"...preach [proclaim] the Kingdom..."* (Luke 9:60).

We must see this as the hour and season of the Kingdom of God! The Kingdom of God is the Rule of God. He alone rules the nations. This must be the season that we rest, serve and operate within the reign of the Kingdom of God. God alone rules over all! He rules over sickness, poverty, demons, sin, and defeat. We must refuse to look back, for those who do are not fit (appropriate, meet) for the Kingdom (rule, reign, realm) of God (Luke 9:62). This is why some are not seeing victory in their walk and work, because they are looking back. Make the King and His Kingdom the priority of your life.

> *"...seek ye first the Kingdom..."* (Matthew 6:33).

Kingdom living is being filled with and led by the Holy Spirit! The Word of God is the constitution of the Kingdom and the Holy Spirit is the power of the Kingdom. Apart from Him we will have no life, hope or strength for this hour.

<u>Pursue a greater understanding of who you are designed and ordained to be in Christ Jesus</u>. Only in Him do we live, exist, move, operate, succeed, and have our being.

> *"For in him we live, and move, and have our being..."* (Acts 17:28a).

Our lives are hid in Him.

> *"For ye are dead, and your life is hid with Christ in God"* (Colossians 3:3).

We have entered the season where deception and misinformation is common. The enemy is causing many to faint and fail through his lies of distorted identity. Our identity in Jesus Christ is most essential to our daily victory. If we can be talked out of or away from who we are in Christ, we can be defeated. The Body of Christ must know, recognize and walk in the finished work of Jesus Christ, which determines and establishes our new identity. The very first temptation that Jesus faced from Satan in the wilderness was one of His identity. This setting is recorded in Matthew 3:17 to 4:3. At the close of chapter 3, the Father is recorded as saying:

"This is My beloved Son, in whom I am well pleased."

We know this setting is the water baptism of Jesus in the Jordan River by John the Baptist. Then we read in verse 1 of chapter 4 that the Holy Spirit leads Jesus into the wilderness to be tempted of the devil. The devil's first temptation was one of identity.

"...if thou be the Son of God, command that these stones be made bread" (Matthew 4:3).

Note the words, "if thou be the Son of God." The Father said that Jesus was His beloved Son. The enemy will tempt us with a similar statement, "if you be born of God; if you are truly saved; if you are right with God."

It is so critically important that each of us get a current relevant revelation of who we are in Jesus Christ. We must know without any doubt that we are born of God, redeemed by the blood of Jesus Christ. You, my dear friend must know without a doubt that you are made the righteousness of God in Christ Jesus. You must be fully persuaded and thoroughly assured in your heart that you are born into son-ship in Christ, reconciled to the Father through Jesus Christ, and made fully complete in Him who is your Lord.

Propose to see life differently. We must seek to see life and circumstances from a new perspective. How we see things determines how we respond to them. We will need to see life, difficulties, trials, and circumstances from God's point of view. Those with the right perspective are not easily moved. In this season we will need to see difficulties and trials as opportunities to be a living witness. We in the western church world often see trials and testing as the results of some failure or sin on our part; but we know according to God's Word that is not always the case. The Apostle Paul and Silas make a great example of those who were faced with a painful difficulty, but used it as an opportunity for Christ Jesus. Recorded in Acts 16, Paul and Silas were ministering the gospel in Philippi where they casted a demon out of a young girl. The master of the girl, who had been using her for profit, was outraged that the demon was cast out and the possible financial gain was gone, so he had Paul and Silas brought before the magistrate. The town magistrate had Paul and Silas beaten and cast into jail.

The magistrate charged the jailer to keep them firmly. The jailer put them in the inner jail. Paul and Silas could have taken the attitude that so many take today and became bitter and angry with God. But, they did not! At midnight, Paul and Silas were heard by the other prisoners singing and praising God. From that an earthquake occurred and tore open the jail. The jailer came in thinking all had escaped and was ready to kill himself. Paul assured him that they were all there. The jailer fell down before Paul and Silas and asked, "What must I do to be saved?" Glory to the Most High! Paul and Silas' attitudes towards a hardship and trial became a cartelist for the jailer and his household to get saved.

What and how we see difficulties and trials in this season is critically important to our personal victory. We will need to see everything from an eternal and not a temporal perspective. What are you seeing? Are you seeing beyond your natural sight? It's time to see clearly!

> "...And Elisha prayed, and said, Lord, I pray thee, open his eyes, that he may see. And the Lord opened the eyes of the young man; and he saw..." (Second Kings 6:8-17).

My prayer for the Church of the Living God is that we will see clearly the events and storms as we should. Oh Lord, open our eyes to see clearly. Jesus counsels the church of Laodicea in Revelation 3:17,18 to come to Him that He might anoint their eyes with eye salve, that they may see. The last church age of Revelation had an urgent need to see accurately and clearly. This is where the church of the 21st century is today—in need of clear and accurate sight.

Prepare for change. Old mentalities and rigid mindsets may break. Adapt, adjust and improvise. Life, circumstances and the world may experience great change—will you adjust accordingly? I must admit that I have been one who does enjoy consistency and stability. Change has often come with some resistance. My wife and children are at times challenging me to let go of old methods and adjust to newness. I fully agree, but agreeing has not made it necessarily easier. I am not one to change things just for the sake of change. I am not one who quickly jumps on the wagon just because others say we should. I am fully and thoroughly resistant to joining the crowd of this evil world system just because it becomes popular. It has been my commitment to live a set apart life unto Jesus Christ and not according to the dictates of this world system. However, there are some changes that are needful and unavoidable. I believe that the Spirit of God is encouraging us to prepare our minds and lives for undeniable change. The judgment of sin is upon our nation. The consequences of our choices have come to harvest. The outcomes of personal, social and political choices will create a world and nation unlike anything we have ever known. I am hearing from the Spirit of the Living God, "Prepare for change!"

Prepare to fight. Fight the good fight of faith. Fight against the doubts and unbelief that will attempt to destroy your confidence in God.

> *"Fight the good fight of faith, lay hold on eternal life..."* (First Timothy 6:12).

Fight for what is most important to you. Nehemiah and the nation of Judah were commanded to fight against the enemies of God that attempted to hinder the rebuilding of the wall there in Jerusalem.

> *"...fight for your brethren, your sons, and your daughters, your wives, and your houses"* (Nehemiah 4:14).

Anything worth having is worth fighting for. We must be willing to stand firm and fight for the values that once made this nation great. Fight for the eternal souls of humanity. When I look into the eyes of my children and grandchildren I hear deep within my heart a warrior's cry, "Fight!" There are a number of things in this life that I will fight for until the end; my family, faith and friends are on the top of that list. What are you willing to fight for? Are there things you are willing to give your life for?

We are not fighting this fight of faith alone! We are not fighting a losing battle! Know that we are not fighting this fight ill-equipped. Know that God will fight for you in this battle.

> *"Be strong and courageous, be not afraid nor dismayed...With him is an arm of flesh; but with us is the Lord our God to help us, and to fight our battles..."* (Second Chronicles 32:7,8); *"...For we wrestle not against flesh and blood, but against principalities...against spiritual wickedness in high places..."* (Ephesians 6:10-13).

I have often said, "I can handle just about anything in life just as long as I am sure that God is with me." Brothers and sisters we can be fully assured in the battles that lay ahead of us that the Lord is with us. He will never leave us nor forsake us. If God be for you, who can stand against you? Identify your enemy and the direction of your fight. You are not shadow boxing, but there is a real opponent.

> *"...not as uncertainly; so fight I, not as one that beateth the air..."* (First Corinthians 9:24-27).

This enemy is a relentless foe who has come to steal, kill and destroy anything and everything of God in your life. Never give up, decline to give in, and refuse to give out.

Refuse to live in fear. An effective military tactic of an enemy has been to create fear in the hearts of his opponent. When fear enters the heart the will to fight is greatly diminished. Internal fear is a formula for personal defeat. Fear saps our energy and nullifies our creativity. Fear in the heart is a sign to the inner man that faith is greatly needed. Fear of the enemy is a signal that faith in God is required. Take whatever time is needed to cultivate and activate faith in God's means and ability to assure your victory. Address and face the fear before entering the battle. Fear is an inside image of a possible or pending failure. Fear has confidence of a future defeat, harm or failure. Fear is a choice, therefore refuse to fear.

"...Be not ye afraid of them: remember the Lord, which is great and terrible..." (Nehemiah 4:14).

The prepared and ready are less likely to be gripped and accosted by fear. The Lord has not given us a spirit of fear; we have a spirit of power, love, and a sound mind. We must be assured in our hearts that God loves us and will care for us, no matter what we face. With this attitude fear has no resting place in us.

"...There is no fear in love; but perfect love casteth out fear..." (First John 4:17,18).

Don't give up, don't give in, don't look back, and don't stop. We must be determined to keep moving toward the victory we have been given in Christ Jesus. Press toward your goals and dreams. Refuse to be stopped. Refuse to waste time complaining or making excuses. Press forward!

"...forgetting those things which are behind, and reaching forth unto those things which are before, I press toward the mark..." (Philippians 3:13,14).

Refuse to faint in this journey. I have noticed more and more believers who started this journey of faith falling and fainting in their walk. Hold fast to your faith in Christ. Hold fast to the gifts and calling that Christ has entrusted to you. The race is not given to the swift nor to the strong, but to those who endure unto the end. You must finish your race! Finish well what you have been graced with, for the reward is given to those who finish and to those who overcome.

Wisdom to Remember: Prepare is the optimum word, preparation is never wasted time, and the unprepared are disqualified!

Chapter Six

THERE IS REST, PROVISION, SAFETY, AND THE BLESSING TO THE PEOPLE OF GOD!

"He redeemed us in order that the blessing given to Abraham might come to the Gentiles through Christ Jesus, so that by faith we might receive the promise of the Spirit."
(Galatians 3:14) (NIV)

The Rested Life. The Lord has called us to live and labor from the vantage point of rest. As much of the world face continued unrest we who are in Christ Jesus must affirm that we are appointed to a life free of fear and anxiety, a place called "Rest." The writer of Hebrews gives us tremendous insight into this rest of God. It is recorded in Hebrews 4:9-11:

"There remaineth therefore a rest to the people of God. For he that is entered into his rest, he also hath ceased from his own works, as God did from His. Let us labor therefore to enter into that rest,

lest any man fall after the same example of unbelief."

Wow, what a powerful word! Jesus Christ is our resting place! He is also the land in which we are to enter and find rest for our souls. As God rested on the seventh day from His labor we are to abide in the seventh day of rest that we have in Jesus Christ. We are to cease from our own labors.

In these last days we are to labor to enter and remain in this rest that we have been given in Jesus. We must discontinue attempting to do life our own way. We must no longer attempt to live life or serve God without Him. Yes, most of the world has sought to live life without the consciousness and awareness of God. Many of the world's religions are no more than human ingenuity to self governing their lives without God. The rest of God cannot be gained by more human efforts; it can only be obtained by yielding and surrendering fully to God's eternal plan. His name is Jesus Christ! As we enter into a genuine, loving, biblical relationship with God the Father through the finished work of Jesus Christ, we then enter into the rest of God. That rest is then affirmed and matured through our faith and understanding of who He is and who we are in Him.

Dear friends, grow in this rest that you have been given in Christ. Though the world may be coming apart at the seams, we who are born of God in Christ Jesus are given a rest. This rest that is given to the people of God will transcend political unrest, economic upheaval, and social disorder. As Jesus rested in the boat as the disciples rowed franticly, so we too must locate that given rest. We are to rest in God's Word that assures us safe passage to the other side.

> "...Many are the afflictions of the righteous: but the Lord delivereth him out of them all" (Psalm 34:17-19); "I sought the Lord, and he heard me, and delivered me from all my fears...This poor man cried, and the Lord heard him, and saved him out of all his troubles" (Psalm 34:4,6).

We are not appointed unto the wrath and judgment of God. As I have stated earlier, what the nations are about to experience are out of man's own choosing.

> "For God hath not appointed us to wrath, but to obtain salvation by our Lord Jesus Christ," (First Thessalonians 5:9).

We can be confident and assured that God is for us and not against us. The Lord is our refuge, safety, peace, rest, and fortress.

> "...He is my refuge and my fortress: my God; in Him will I trust..." (Psalm 91:1-16).

We are to rest in the grace of God. In this season this kind of rested living is an absolute must. In Christ Jesus our covenant and care is finished and affirmed. God's eternal grace is more than sufficient for us. His strength is made perfect and complete in our weakness. The grace of God is the favor, might, ability, means, strength, and resources of the Most High God. This grace is to be God's ability, producing in His church and in His people stress-less labor; stress-less labor that is anchored in the hearts of a people devoted to total obedience to the Word and will of God. This stress-less labor is lead and directed by the Person of the Holy Spirit. The Lord tells the Apostle Paul in Second Corinthians 12:7-10:

> "...My grace is sufficient for thee: for my strength is made perfect in weakness..."

Grace in the Greek equals Charis (khar'-ece) graciousness, acceptable, benefit, favor, gift, joy liberality, pleasure.[6]

As I have examined and studied grace I understand grace as the limitless means, ability, provisions, and favor of God fully and freely bestowed upon another through the eternal covenant found in Jesus Christ the Anointed. We have access to the Grace of God through the eternal ministry of Jesus Christ.

> *"...one grace after another and spiritual blessing upon spiritual blessing and even favor upon favor and gift [heaped] upon gift. For while the Law was given through Moses, grace (unearned, undeserved favor and spiritual blessing) and truth came through Jesus Christ"* (St. John 1:16,17) (Amplified).

God's grace does not negate our responsibilities. Be assured we cannot turn a deaf ear to grace or it would no longer be grace. The disciplines of the Christian faith are a part of our responsibilities and they are not an attempt to move God. The disciplines are our portion in growing and maturing our faith and obedience towards God. We groom our hearts in faith through the disciplines. Disciplines (prayer, fasting, reading the Word, meditation of the Word, fellowship, witnessing, church attendance, and serving) along with the ministering work of the Holy Spirit are necessary to maintain a consistent life of faith towards God. We do not earn grace through our daily disciplines; we respond to grace through our disciplines.

There is nothing we can do to move or manipulate God. He has already moved through His Word and His Son Jesus. Yet, God's goodness and grace does respond to faith, desire and obedience.

"Draw nigh to God, and he will draw nigh to you..." (James 4:8).

Grace is God's response to faith in Christ Jesus. God's grace operates through and by the finished work of Jesus Christ. We can do nothing by human effort to earn or qualify for His grace. Faith and obedience is our portion and posture before God that gives His grace place to respond. Rest in the full sufficiency of God's eternal grace!

<u>You are blessed and not cursed</u>. Embrace "The Blessing In Christ Jesus!" Church, know that you are the blessed of the Lord and never cursed. You, who are born of God, are the blessed seed of Abraham. Blessing in the Greek is Eulogia (you-log-ee'-ah) defined as fine speaking, benediction, consecration,

benefit, a bounty of blessings, eulogy.[7] The eulogy is the final declaration of praise of one's life at their death. The Lord has eulogized our lives with high praise, blessing and favor.

> *"He redeemed us in order that the blessing given to Abraham might come to the Gentiles through Christ Jesus, so that by faith we might receive the promise of the Spirit"* (Galatians 3:14) (NIV).

Blessing in Hebrew is brakah (ber-aw-kaw') which means benediction, prosperity.[8]

> *"The blessing of the Lord, it maketh rich, and he addeth no sorrow with it"* (Proverbs 10:22).

The acceptance of Jesus Christ our Savior and Lord, with His divine covenant, accompanied with faith, a life of obedience to God and His Word, actives the Blessing. We can be saved by God, but live alienated from the Blessings of God. Some have chosen to live estranged to their blessing, by living in unbelief and disobedience; yet we must believe that we who are in Christ Jesus have been graced with "The Blessing."

> *"....if thou shalt hearken diligently unto the Voice of the Lord thy God, to observe and to do*

all his commandments which I command thee
this day...all these blessing shall come on thee,
and overtake thee,..." (Deuteronomy 28:1-14).

A Spoken Blessing

I decree, declare and proclaim "The Blessing" of the Lord Jesus upon you.

- The Blessing of the Lord shall forever remove and eradicate every lying, destructive, and nonproductive word ever spoken against you.
- The Blessing of the Lord has uprooted, dislodged, and dispelled every demonic curse, hex, voodoo or spell array against your life.
- The Blessing of the Lord has made you exceedingly rich and there will be no sorrow with it.
- The Blessing of the Lord shall continue to overtake you.
- The Blessing of the Lord has bestowed upon you spiritual eyes to see and spiritual ears to hear.
- The Blessing of the Lord has favored you in the city, increased you in the field, and prospered you in your travels.

- The Blessing of the Lord has restored your body with good health, strength, vitality, and endurance.
- The Blessing of the Lord has renewed your mind to think clearly and soundly. The mind of Christ is operational in you. You are blessed to be innovative, creative, wise, knowledgeable, and insightful in all things in life.
- The Blessing of the Lord has activated and generated uncommon favor with God and man.
- The Blessing of the Lord has opened doors that no man can close and closed doors that no man can open.
- The Blessing of the Lord shall cause you to be fruitful and prosperous in everything you put your hands to.
- The Blessing of the Lord shall multiply you when you come in and increase you when you leave out.
- The Blessing of the Lord shall make you plenteous in goods, to the abundant overflow.
- The Blessing of the Lord has produced wealth, riches and success in you to the degree that you will always have sufficiency to give to every good work.

- The Blessing of the Lord shall cause you to be a lender and not a borrower.
- The Blessing of the Lord has established you as God's holy, set apart, consecrated vessel.
- The Blessing of the Lord shall make you the head and never the tail, above and never beneath.
- The Blessing of the Lord shall cause you to over-come and be victorious in all things.
- The Blessing of the Lord has commissioned angelic assistance, care and protection as one who is an heir of salvation.
- You are (I am) forever blessed and never cursed. Embrace the Blessing!

Amen! I encourage you to speak such powerful words over your life and the life of your family each day. As the storm clouds mount about the nations it will be imperative that those who are born of God affirm that we are blessed and never cursed.

Wisdom to Remember: True rest is a matter of the heart and not the condition of one's circumstances!

Chapter Seven

ESTABLISH AND IMPLEMENT AN EMERGENCY READINESS PLAN

"Where there is no counsel, the people fall; But in the multitude of counselors there is safety." (Proverbs 11:14) (NKJV)

An Emergency Readiness Plan is a guideline to thrive and survive during times of difficulty and disaster. Some reading this portion of the book may quickly say, "We don't need that because God will take care of us." Yes, He certainly will and in doing so He has given us wisdom and understanding. The wisdom and understanding of the Lord commands us to prepare and equip ourselves for what He has made aware to us. I do not believe for one moment that proper preparation is a lack of trust and faith in God. I believe that it is foolish to see and hear the warnings and refuse to equip and prepare ourselves in every way possible. I have communicated in previous chapters the importance of preparing spiritually, emotionally, socially, and psychologically. There must also be some practical and logistical readiness as well. This practical readiness is to be termed, the "Emergency Readiness Plan."

I understand that my words may sound a little like the "doomsday" prophets declaring the end of the world; or perhaps somewhat like those selling products and goods to hide from the end of the world. My efforts are by no means an attempt to create fear, nor to sell you a survival kit to hide away until the end. However, in the midst of all the fear mongering, miscommunications, lies, and deception there is much practical wisdom and insight we can gain from others for this season.

The Emergency Readiness Plan is a practical approach to the events that are set before us and should be written in a simple, easy to understand language. This plan must be regularly updated and easily accessible for implementation. It is my belief that every family, church and community should have a readiness plan in place in order to address an emergency, disaster, and/or economic fallout. I have implemented some aspect of this plan for my home and church. As a father and a pastor I have a responsibility to provide and protect my family and congregation to the very best of my ability. For some, this level of preparation may not appear important or it may appear un-necessary because it is not spiritual enough. We must bring along side and accompany our spiritual readiness with meaningful natural preparedness.

Each family should have an Emergency Readiness Plan that works for them. This plan should spell out how the family intends to address the various challenges that may confront them:

- What will your family do if there is a financial failure and you cannot get to cash, or your debit and/or credit cards will not work?
- What will you do if a local or national security threat is believed to be imminent?
- If there are adult children living outside the family home, will they all meet at the family home?
- How will you provide for your family if all public utility services such as water, power, sewage, and gas suddenly fail?

Your Emergency Readiness Plan needs to spell out your strategy to address these and many other questions.

It is my belief that local churches need to also create and implement such a plan. The leadership of the local church must equip, inform and make ready those under their leadership for the possibilities of difficulty. There should be decisive guidelines on how the local church intends to address a crisis. The readiness plan should communicate to the congregation what support will be available and how to access it. The church should also prepare its plan to address the community's needs at large. If there is a major crisis much of the community will attempt to come to the local church for assistance, even as many do today. The church must address ahead of time the logistical issues in responding to those needs.

The Emergency Readiness Plan will need to address several important factors. The first is spiritual readiness of your family. The individual and entire family should affirm their faith and confidence in God's ability to care and provide for them here today and for eternity. Certainly the adult family heads should lead the family in this assurance as early and as often as possible. I would recommend daily family devotions to prepare the family for a greater trust and dependency upon the grace of God. During your family times, talk about resting and trusting in the

Lord for caring and protecting the family. The worst time to attempt to prepare for a crisis is in the midst of the crisis. As I shared with some in the past, "the worst time to attempt to purchase fire insurance is when the home is on fire!" Honestly ask yourself, "If a major emergency occurred today, would my family be spiritually grounded enough to handle it in faith?"

Secondly, ensure that your family is <u>emotionally, psychologically and mentally ready</u>. This area of readiness is powerfully important. As a former Marine and Law Enforcement Officer, I was trained and taught that emotional trauma and psychological shock can kill as deadly as bullets. I understand that we can never be fully prepared for the shock, pain and heartache, but we can minimize its damage through preparation. I recall responding to a shooting incident (as a Police Officer that affirms just how deadly shock can be) where there was a dispute between two men over a family matter. One man shot the other from a distance of about ten to fifteen yards away with a twelve-gauge shotgun and the victim ran down the street for about two blocks. The victim was shot in the upper chest and face area. When I arrived at the scene where the shooting victim was laying, he had expired. I looked at him carefully and determined (from my point of view) none of his wounds appeared to have been life threatening. So, why was he dead? I believe the shock of being shot caused him to yield to death. He believed he was going to die, and he did. As a Marine infantryman and a Law Enforcement Officer, one learns quickly that the will to live is vital to survival when shot or injured. You must believe you are going to survive. You must not give in to your injuries. An individual's emotional, psychological and mental readiness is a matter of life and death. The shock of change can cause many to give up and perish. A family needs to spend some time discussing and preparing for change. How will they manage if the conveniences of life are suddenly removed? How will your family handle the awareness of a terrorist attack or multiple deaths in your community? Again, I reiterate that none of us can fully prepare for such, but some degree of readiness is extremely important. Many of our service men and women suffer from the effects and experience of combat, medically called Post Traumatic Stress Disorder. The shocking events of war, disasters and devastation are very real, and do cause some to shut down to the point of non-effectiveness.

Thirdly, our families must have some degree of health, physical and fitness readiness. If what we are hearing from the Lord does occur, it certainly will be critically important to have our families as healthy and physically fit as possible. I say this knowing that many families, even now, face medical concerns and some health challenges. However, preparing as best you can will be extremely important if your family will need to relocate quickly; or, if members in your home will have to walk for miles at any given time, their physical readiness will be vital. I would highly recommend some physical fitness training and readiness for every home. Exercising four to five days a week now will go a long way in the days and years to come. Each family should be doing all that is possible to get into the very best physical condition, as feasible. Please do not neglect your children's health and fitness preparation as well. I recommend that parents help their children to do some exercise a few times each week. With fitness readiness there must also be a shift to a healthier diet. Even now there should be a greater commitment to reduce the sugars and soft drinks. In our home we are working to eat foods higher in protein with less fat. Our goal continues to be more fruits and vegetables, and less processed foods.

The fourth area to prepare for is <u>financial readiness</u>. It has been reported by many that a considerable number of the American people are most concerned about the economy above and beyond anything else. In times of disaster and difficulty, economic and financial readiness is imperative to survival. How will we get provisions and supplies if the supermarkets are closed? What will we do if all banking services are suspended? I am neither an economic advisor nor a financial planner; however, I do have some wisdom and insight to the practical matters of life. Therefore, one of the first things I would recommend is to put aside two to four months of cash. Why cash? If there is a major financial shift, then your electronic banking systems may not work. If you have some cash on hand, you will have something to do business with for a few weeks. During the Great Depression of the 1930's one of the first failures was the banking systems. There was a quick run on all cash. Many believe not only should we have months of cash, but other negotiable resources, such as gold and silver. It is my conviction that we must not only have some cash, and perhaps gold and silver on hand, but also make every effort to limit and minimize all debt. During financial difficulties debt becomes a great weight and an unseemly burden. We have also seen with the American housing market just how painful debt can be. Many Americans have found that this present economic season has been most troublesome partly because of excessive debt. With the increase of unemployment and under-employment, lost of savings and mounting inflation, many families have lost their most valuable passion—their homes. One might think that during such a season banks and lenders would exercise great patience with their customers; but no, foreclosures are at an all time high. Make every effort today to minimize any and all debt. Generally speaking, "What you own cannot be taken away."

The fifth area of the plan is <u>operational readiness</u>. It is the practical how, who and where of our readiness plan. Write out your operational readiness plan prescribing who will do what in your family. (Who has what responsibilities of food, cooking, water, utilities, and security?) If your readiness plan is not written out, then it is not a real plan; it is merely a wish list. Ensure that a paper copy of your plan is also stored, as to ensure that you have clear direction if your computers fail. Create and organize a thorough supply list. Identify where those supplies will be stored. Operational readiness is practical implementation of your Emergency Readiness Plan.

The sixth and last area of the Emergency Readiness Plan is security. This area for many seems to be extreme and over the top. If we are truly going to be prepared and ready for the multiple possibilities, then personal, family and community security is a must. Each person and family head must identify and affirm their family's security readiness. I am not by any means advocating violence, but you must be prepared to protect your family and loved ones. We must decide where our personal limits are when it comes to security. Each family head must assess with their family to what limit are they willing to go and to what level of force are they committed to use in order to protect their loved ones from crime and violence.

If weapons of any kind are to be stored with the intent to use if needed, then I highly recommend that all of the adults in your family complete a weapons safety class. I believe there may be a day when we will have to defend our families, homes, churches, and communities with force. As I shared earlier, each individual and family should decide their own level of security for themselves. Each must let their own faith and conscious guide them. I settled the self-defense and handgun issue years ago while serving as a Marine for ten years and a Police Officer for eight and a half years. For me it is not a lack of faith or a failure to trust God when one carries a rifle, handgun, or to be physically prepared to defend themselves or their family. I can hear some of you saying as I pen this, "But how about trusting God to protect you!" And I say, "Yes and Amen!" He does and He will. Yes, He has given His Angels charge to aid and care for us. Having a weapon in your home does not nullify that in my mind. I happen to believe that God can use whatever means He deems necessary to care for and protect me and my family. When Jesus was taken by the Jewish leaders there in the garden they came to Him with swords and staves. It is very interesting that prior to this so-called arrest Jesus instructs His disciples to buy a sword.

> "...he that hath no sword, let him sell his garment, and buy one...And they said, Lord, behold, here are two swords. And he said unto them, It is enough" (Luke 22:35-38).

I must admit this is very unusual communication. However, moments after this Jesus is arrested, but would not let His disciples use the very swords they possessed. Why? Because it was not the right time, that's why. There is a time for everything. Jesus tells His disciples as the Jewish leaders were taking Him:

"...*Suffer ye thus far...*" (Luke 22:51).

Jesus would not let them use force to protect Him because His arrest had to happen in order to fulfill what was written in the scriptures. If He needed help, He had twelve legions of angels to assist.

We must maintain the proper balance between what is our responsibility and what we believe God will take care of. Emotional and mental preparedness greatly increases your ability to survive and to successfully protect your family. I also believe there can be great value in taking a physical self-defense class. What will you do if faced with an attempted carjacking or an armed robbery? We should have some understanding and awareness of what to do in the event of a violent physical assault. I highly recommend that adults and teens learn some basic self-defense strategies.

Here are several general recommendations that will assist you in creating and implementing an effective Emergency Readiness Plan:

1. Singles and single parents may want to create and organize their plan with another single or single parent. The supplies and demands upon each may require the combined efforts of a few. Battle planning and implementation of any sort is best done in a team and group environment.

2. Create a location where you will store your family food supply and other necessary items. I suggest using a garage, an extra bedroom or closet. Based on the size of your family you will need to store supplies proportionately. I would advise a family to store no less than thirty days of food and water.

3. You will need to create a supplemental cooking source for your home. This should be determined ahead of time and not delayed.

4. How will you heat your home if the regular heating system fails in the midst of winter? I recommend that you determine what that will be as soon as possible. If you have a fireplace, then locating a good supply of firewood is important. If a fireplace is not possible, perhaps

a kerosene heater may be an alternative. Even if you do not set these systems up, having them in place or stored in case they are needed is a great idea.

The U.S. Department of Homeland Security has a list of items that can be a tremendous aid in your preparation. They encourage all Americans to take some steps to prepare for and respond to potential emergencies. Their website (www.ready.gov) will assist you in putting that list together. It appears to be a very useful resource. I strongly urge you to carefully read the material and recommendations given. A well thought out supply list is extremely valuable. Listed below are some of the items that are recommended for each family to have on hand:

- One gallon of water per person, per day for at least three days for drinking and sanitation; and at least a three-day supply of non-perishable food
- Battery-powered or hand crank radio and a NOAA weather radio with tone alert, and extra batteries for both
- Flashlight and extra batteries
- First aid kit

- Whistle to signal for help
- Dust mask (to help filter contaminated air), plastic sheeting and duct tape to keep shelter-in-place
- Moist towelettes, garbage bags and plastic ties for personal sanitation
- Wrench or pliers to turn off utilities
- Can opener for food (if kit contains canned food)
- Local maps
- Cell phone and chargers
- Prescription medications and glasses
- Infant formula and diapers
- Pet food and extra water for your pet
- Important family documents such as copies of insurance policies, identification and bank account records in a waterproof, portable container
- Cash or traveler's checks and change
- Emergency reference material such as a first aid book
- Sleeping bag or warm blanket for each person; consider additional bedding if you live in a cold-weather climate

- Complete change of clothing including a long sleeved shirt, long pants and sturdy shoes
- Household chlorine bleach and medicine dropper (When diluted nine parts water to one part bleach, bleach can be used as a disinfectant; or, in an emergency, you can use it to treat water by using sixteen drops of regular household liquid bleach per gallon of water. Do not use scented, color safe or bleaches with added cleaners.)
- Fire Extinguisher
- Matches in a waterproof container
- Feminine supplies and personal hygiene items
- Toilet paper for two weeks
- Mess kits, paper cups, paper plates, plastic utensils, and paper towels
- Paper and pencil, books, games, puzzles or other activities for children

Wisdom to Remember: The wise and insightful purchases flood insurance long before the first rain drop falls.

Chapter Eight

CAN THE UNIMAGINABLE HAPPEN AGAIN IN AMERICA?

"Be not deceived; God is not mocked: for whatsoever a man soweth, that shall he also reap." (Galatians 6:7)

America the Beautiful. Many years ago there was a popular television commercial that showed the wearied face of a Native American looking and viewing the state of the American landscape. As he witnessed the litter, pollution and crowded highways, you could see a single tear falling down his cheek. The commercial left you with the idea that America had lost much of the beauty and splendor of its founded past.

What would be the reaction of President George Washington to the present state of America? What would he and the many other founding leaders of this great republic say about the present state of this nation? In President George Washington's Inaugural address to both Houses of Congress on April 30, 1789 he states, "We ought to be no less persuaded that the propitious smiles of Heaven can never be expected on a nation that disregards the eternal rules of order and right which Heaven itself has ordained; and since the preservation of that sacred fire of liberty and the destiny of the republican model of government are justly considered as deeply, perhaps finally, staked of the experiment."[9] I believe that America has consistently abandoned the spiritual, moral and social values that graced its beginning. I would suspect that George Washington would have far more than a single tear rolling down his cheek if he was permitted to see the present state of America. I am sure he would be amazed by the countless scientific achievements and awed by the global military dominance; but, America had and has a far greater purpose than science and might. There once was an America that was committed to Christian liberties, political justice, personal freedom, and human rights.

The Unimaginable. In 2000, a disaster film titled "The Perfect Storm" was released. The movie starred George Clooney and Mark Wahlberg and centered on a fishing expedition of the famed ship and crew called the "Andrea Gail." While on an urgent fishing adventure the ship and crew are faced with the dilemma of navigating through two powerful weather fronts and a forming hurricane. The movie seemed to convey to its audience a number of life lessons, some of which are: there are numerous perils in life, there are pains to those who make ill-advised choices, and yes, there are countless sorrows to those who ignore the warning signs of pending danger. At the end of the movie the ship and much of the crew are lost in the storm.

There are times in human history when events, conditions and unimaginable circumstances all converge upon a single period of time, and there history is re-directed. I believe America has come to such a place and season in time; and the perfect storm is upon us. For generations the wicked hearts of men, unrighteous pursuits of the masses, and political corruption of some of our leaders have all helped generate the perfect conditions for a horrific season of difficulty. Yes, we now face the perfect storm! America has forsaken the God that made it great; the same God that we once honored by printing on our currency the famed words, "In God We Trust!" Who do we trust today?

Strong and great nations do not come into existence strictly by the will of men, but by the gracious hand of Almighty God.

> *"Uprightness and right standing with God (moral and spiritual rectitude in every area and relation) elevate a nation, but sin is a reproach to any people"* (Proverbs 14:34) (Amplified).

One of the most revealing scriptures about this approaching storm is found in Psalm 9:17:

> *"The wicked shall be turned into hell, and all the nations that forget God..."*

God is no respecter of any; what is just for one is just for all. The nation of Israel faced the pains of their choice when they forsook the God of their fathers. From that choice they were defeated by their enemies, taken captive, and exiled to Babylon for seventy years. Pride and arrogance would compel a people to say within themselves that "such devastation can never happen to us." There have been many great civilizations that have faced critical crossroads as America now faces, and they chose wrongly and ceased to be a dominant global nation. There have been foreboding and ominous nations such as Egypt, Persia, Greece, and Rome, that all eventually fell to internal and external forces. Nineveh was also such a nation—a nation that was facing pending judgment from God.

> *"Arise, go to Nineveh, that great city, and cry against it; for their wickedness is come up before me"* (Jonah 1:2).

As it was with Nineveh, the sin and wickedness of a nation and people rises up before a holy and righteous God. When Jonah finally arrived and preached repentance to the nation of Nineveh they repented.

> *"And Jonah began to enter into the city a day's journey, and he cried, and said, Yet forty days, and Nineveh shall be overthrown. So the people of Nineveh believed God, and proclaimed a fast, and put on sackcloth, from the greatest of them even to the least of them. For word came unto the king of Nineveh, and he arose from his throne, and he laid his robe from him, and covered him with sackcloth, and sat in ashes…"* (Jonah 3:4-7).

Then, in verse 10 we read of God's response to their repentance:

> *"And God saw their works, that they turned from their evil way; and God repented of the evil,*

that he had said that he would do unto them; and he did it not."

As we witnessed in the September 11th terrorist attacks and in the Hurricane Katrina disaster, America is no longer exempted from the pains, difficulties and sorrows of its unrighteous choices. Without the Divine Creator's gracious care and compassionate protection we are most vulnerable to the perfect storm. America's perfect storm can be a combination of one, two and/or many foreseeable factors. Any one of the following conditions discussed can trigger national fallout.

The saturation of sin and immorality certainly can and often is a trigger that activates the conditions for a perfect storm of difficulty upon a nation. As we read earlier of the nation of Nineveh, it was their wickedness that activated the judgment of God. Let's make a point very clear: judgment is already upon sin and does not require God to do anything. Sin is already judged. The wages of sin is death, but the gift of God is eternal life. God needs not to sit upon His glorious throne in heaven and declare judgment upon nations and souls. He declared from the beginning to Adam and Eve, "the day you sin you shall surely die!" Just like water carries with it wet, so sin carries judgment. Sin is the transgression of the divine law of our Creator God. America has consistently moved further and further from the biblical standards of righteousness. Our moral code has moved further from God's eternal truth.

The American culture has consistently attempted to redefine what right and wrong is. A number of American States have gone to the ballot box in an attempt to protect marriage. In North Carolina where I reside, a State Constitution Amendment was passed that states marriage in this State is only recognized between one man and one woman. I was grateful that the Amendment did pass; but why would that ever be a question? Unfortunately, it is a question because of the rise of the spirit of Sodom that has attempted to change the natural truth of nature into something vile and corrupt. Marriage was and is God's idea and His plan for the family.

> *"Therefore shall a man leave his father and his mother, and shall cleave unto his wife: and they shall be one flesh"* (Genesis 2:24).

That verse is so very clear to me! Sin and immorality does and will activate consequences and judgment upon a person and upon a nation. There is a supreme law that governs the earth. If we use that law in righteous obedience, it will generate and produce grace and blessings. However, if we live vile, wicked lives, that law will produce accordingly. It is called the law of sowing and reaping. What we sow is what we will also reap.

> *"Be not deceived; God is not mocked: for whatsoever a man [nation] soweth; that shall he [they] also reap"* (Galatians 6:7).

The <u>devaluing and taking of human life</u> has positioned America for unparalleled difficulty. The Fifth Commandment says, "Thou shalt not kill." We know that this command from Exodus 20:13 is telling us not to take innocent life. The spirit of murder has risen and saturated much of our nation like a cancer. To Almighty God human life has supreme and eternal value. There is no human right more precious and no gift more sacred than life. We read of the first murder in Genesis 4, there Cain killed his brother, Abel. In verse 10 the Lord said:

> *"...the voice of thy brother's blood crieth unto me from the ground."*

How much more is the cry of the blood of the millions upon millions of souls murdered in this nation and around the world?

The greatest American tragedy ever permitted upon this land has been the taking of human life through legalized abortion. It is believed and reported by some that since the passing of Roe v. Wade in January 1973, over sixty million babies' lives have been terminated here in America. Surely, the blood of those innocent lives has cried out unto a holy and just God. According to the Center for Disease Control, thirty-four percent of all abortions in America are performed on the African American female. It has also been reported that the leading cause of death amongst African Americans is abortion. The only population group in America that is in numerical decline is African Americans. Genocide is taking place in America through legalized abortion. Their cry for justice is heard in heaven and the storm clouds of judgment are approaching.

America is also faced with the growing assault upon the aged and elderly. It appears that many insurance companies and governmental agencies are searching far more diligently for creative ways to euthanize the elderly than to help cure them. Their blood cries out for justice alongside our unborn. I am hearing the sound of a storm approaching!

Our communities, schools and homes are consistently faced with the images and assaults of a society given unto <u>lawlessness, crime and violence</u>. Crime and corruption seem to have invaded every institution of our land. Our local and national news are inundated with one report after another of greed, hatred, violence, and murder. The condition of our present age brings to mind the words of Jesus when He said:

> *"...as it was in the days of Noah, so shall it be also in the days of the Son of man"* (St. Luke 17:26).

What was it like in Noah's day? In Genesis 6:5 we read:

> *"And God saw that the wickedness of man was great in the earth, and that every imagination of the thoughts of his heart was only evil continually."*

We know and read that God brought judgment upon the earth because of this evil that ran ramped in the earth. The American jails and prisons are incarcerating more and more inmates each year, yet crime and violence continues to be on the increase. Our judicial systems are strained to capacity. With such strain far too many are being wrongly imprisoned, creating a whole new problem. Our prisons no longer use the term rehabilitation; now it's imprison and throw away the key. The great nation of the United States of America is one of the leading nations in the entire world with one of the highest number of imprisoned citizens. The American judicial system is said to be one of the best of the world, yet far too many citizens are being wrongfully imprisoned. Our State and Federal governments continue to pass frivolous laws year after year that have made our nation a nation of criminals. Our continued lawlessness, crime and violence are summoning upon our land judgment and a curse. Lord, have mercy upon America!

Our nation has gotten a small taste of the chaos and confusion that a Timothy McVeigh and Terry Nichols can cause (McVeigh and Nichols were convicted of the Oklahoma City Bombing of April 1995), but most of us could not imagine the level of difficulty and mayhem a dirty bomb could cause to the normal operations of our nation. The continued threat of terrorism lingers heavily upon the hearts and minds of much of America. New York City,

Washington, D.C. and many other major metropolitan cities are regularly faced with terror threat levels. According to our political leaders, our intelligence agencies are working feverously to identify and stop any future terror assaults upon our land. Many believe that the great threat of future terror assaults may not come from a foreign assailant, but a home grown one. For many Americans, trusting the government to secure our safety and well being has become a great stretch. In 2013, it came to light that the National Security Agency has spent considerable time and resources gathering the personal information of its own citizens. This has aroused much concern for those of us who greatly value personal liberties and individual freedoms.

Perhaps our greater concern need not be for the threat of a dirty bomb from the Middle East, but an aged and worn <u>power grid</u> right here at home. So much of our lives are locked into the availability of electricity. Few American's can operate and function effectively without the all mighty power grid. The impact of a major power failure across our nation could significantly disrupt commerce and comfort for us all. Many in the energy industry believe that our present power grid system is in desperate need of an upgrade and repair. However, few are willing to spend the money or take on the mammoth task. Sadly to say, the urgent need for improvements and upgrades could show itself at its most critical time.

The storms of difficulty are mounting and looming over our nation. The growing national financial deficit greatly concerns me as a tax paying citizen. In January 2013, I heard a national renowned economist say that the rising national debt will have little to no impact on the stability of our nation. I thought to myself, "how foolish." Debt of any kind is un-healthy and un-profitable. It is believed that from 2008 to 2012 America's national debt climbed from $7 trillion to over $16 trillion. This is foolish when nearly forty percent of the nation's Gross National Product (GNP) is spent to maintenance this mounting debt. We cannot run our personal finances the way our States and Federal governments run our nation. There will come a day for our nation when pay up is demanded; then, who will be faced with paying the bill and how? Sadly, our children, grandchildren and great grandchildren are faced with a mounting debt that they did not create and certainly will not be able to pay.

The Federalization of America is a threat to the people of America. What do I mean by "Federalization of America?" It means the expansion and takeover of the federal government. On the surface it may look enticing and attractive, but at the end we become a Socialist or Communist state—beware, lest we become a nation that no longer exists for the people and by the people; but, a nation that labors for the existence and sustainability of the government. We have seen how Russia, North Korea and China have all tried to federalize their countries for decades and it has not worked well for them and certainly not for their citizens. I strongly believe that governmental intrusion, governmental expansion and political corruption pose an imminent threat to the sovereignty of America. With mounting growth of government in this country the individual rights and freedoms of our citizens are being diminished more and more each day. I suspect that at some point the American people will wake up, rise up and demand a change. I pray that such change will be brought about peaceably through the ballot box and not forcibly upon our cities and streets.

Increased taxation also poses a critical threat to the safety and well being of our nation. Political and social revoke have occurred to a number of nations when taxation without proper representation occurs. I, like most Americans, believe that proper and reasonable taxation is appropriate and necessary, but when is enough, enough? I feel that we are already seeing some revoke to excessive taxation and mounting governmental regulations through the increased exiting of many American companies. I believe our government has forced many corporations to take their jobs and products to foreign soils. Businesses are in business to make a profit, which creates jobs. When people have employment they can care for their families and pay taxes. As taxation continues to mount, the dangers and difficulties will also mount. The government is not a job creator; free enterprise, entrepreneurship and businesses create jobs and move the economy forward. (Economics 101 teaches us that.) Increased taxation can certainly trigger a major outcry and activate a storm of horrific difficulty.

Growing unemployment and under employment certainly destabilizes our economy and communities. In the years of 2012 through 2014, the national unemployment percentage was about nine percent. What happens to a people who are faced with long term unemployment? Hopelessness, despair, and eventually desolation set in. Hopelessness robs a people and a nation of their dreams and creativity. What becomes of a nation and a people when this becomes the norm for far too many? We have witnessed in the last twenty-five years more and more jobs shift from middle-class blue collar income to minimum wage service industry occupations. For many families two to three incomes per household is now required in order to maintain their basic needs. More American workers are under employed now than any other time in American history. When people feel that they can no longer care for their families they begin to demand change. I can see that the demand for change is rising upon the hearts of many. Prepare for change!

The <u>devaluing of the U.S. Dollar</u> is also a major factor in the instability of America. For a number of years the true worth and value of the U.S. Dollar has consistently dropped. There was a time when the dollar was backed up by a silver and gold certificate, but today the dollar is only backed by the good faith of the U.S. government. With the American debt level passing $16 trillion, that good faith is quickly fading. As America's ability to repay its debt weakens, the value and worth of the dollar loses more and more of its worth. Many nations are moving away from the dollar as its global currency. What will be the outcome and/or fallout of the American economy if the dollar continues to lose its value?

The fall or shifting of global economies has and certainly can cause a rippling effect upon the economics of multiple nations. No one knows the full impact that the struggling Euro can and does have on the American economy. Through instant communications and international investing the world is tied together like never before. The world we live in today is so economically intertwined it makes us all better off, or perhaps worst off. The instability of any part of the world will certainly have some bearing upon the prices paid here at home. We have often seen this very thing played out in the Middle East; as conflicts emerge, global gas prices dramatically fluctuate.

War and military conflict has the potential to redirect a nation like few other things. War has at times promoted a greater level of national pride; but, the pride of nationalism fades quite quickly when our sons and daughters come home in flag draped coffins. As a former active duty Marine, I was honored to serve and certainly willing to give my life for the values and faith that made this nation great. However, as I have matured I find myself more and more concerned about the integrity and clarity of our political leaders who send our service men and women into harm's way with little concern. The U.S. military might is unmatched by any, however, our fading national moral clarity makes America vulnerable in more ways than we could ever know.

America's relationship with Israel has been and is vital to our ongoing favor with God. In Genesis 12:3, the Bible declares that God will bless those who bless Abraham and will curse those who curse Abraham. This blessing extends to our relationship with the nation of Israel as well, with whom America has maintained good relations for decades. The nation of Israel is God's chosen people, the same people that Jesus Christ our Savior came from. I cannot understand how any professed Christian can ever be anti-Semitic, when Jesus Himself was Semitic. This premise of blessing Israel is by no means an open approval of all of Israel's political or military choices; but, all countries need to guard their actions as they address and relate with the nation and people of Israel.

Natural disasters such as floods, fires, hurricanes, drought, and snow can and does change the stability of a nation like no other. Any one of these horrific events can create a life altering setting for a large portion of America, and God forbid any of these triggers coincide. Are we ready and equipped for such a time? I say again, "Prepare!" Some would say that we have always had destructive weather. Yes, but not at this frequency and high level of destruction. The world has faced record number cold winters and hot summers, and the occurrence and devastation of hurricanes in America has steadily increased. Hurricanes Hugo, Andrew, and Katrina (just to name a few) all brought devastation and destruction to many across America. Interesting enough 2012 brought killer fires in the mid-west, drought to the corn States, and much flooding to the east coast. Many call these natural events "Acts of God," yet we know He's not the culprit that causes them. They are the acts of nature! However, I do believe that the earth itself groans and travails for its deliverance from the sin and wickedness of humanity.

"...For we know that the whole creation groaneth and travaileth in pain together until now" (Romans 8:19-22).

I have often wondered just what impact does six thousand years of sin, murder, war, and violence have on the earth in which we live. Jesus said that Hell or Hades was in the heart of the earth (Matthew 12:40). What impact does hell's enlargement and expansion have on our planet's climate?

"...hell hath enlarged herself, and opened her mouth without measure..." (Isaiah 5:14).

Wisdom to Remember: Wish, want and desire does not determine what the harvest will be, but the seed that is sown will! God is not mocked, whatsoever a man or nation sows that he and they will also reap.

Chapter Nine

THE TRYING OF YOUR FAITH

"But if serving the Lord seems undesirable to you, then choose for yourselves this day whom you will serve, whether the gods your ancestors served beyond the Euphrates, or the gods of the Amorites, in whose land you are living. But as for me and my household, we will serve the Lord."
(Joshua 24:15) (NIV)

Our faith, confidence and commitment to the Lord Jesus Christ will face testing and proving in these last hours like we have never witnessed before. We know that the just are called to live by faith. Our faith must reside fully in Jesus Christ and anchored upon His inerrant Word. The believer's walk is one of trial and temptation, but in all of them we can be assured that we are destined to overcome.

"My brethren, count it all joy when ye fall into divers temptations; knowing this, that the trying

of your faith worketh patience. But let patience have her perfect work, that ye may be perfect and entire, wanting nothing" (James 1:2-4).

In the recent years we have witnessed a number of Christian leaders demonstrate character qualities other than what is commanded from God's Holy Word. Far too many of the Lord's gifted leaders have faced some of life's greatest testing and shamefully to say have faltered in those tests. In early 2011, the Holy Spirit revealed to me that 2011 and beyond would be a time and season of exposure and uncovering of the hidden matters of our lives. Those secret things that were unseen would come to light. I believe that the storm conditions that are swirling around us all will continue to expose our heart's true condition. Whatever is going on in the inner man, the true self will be exposed. Pressure applied to a person's life reveals his or her true state. The trying and testing of our faith reveals who or what we truly trust in.

The Word of God that is deposited into our hearts will be tested! When the Lord speaks a truth into our hearts, very often those very words are soon tested in our lives by circumstances, conditions, or "storms."

"Now it came to pass on a certain day, that he went into a ship with his disciples: and he said unto them, Let us go over unto the other side of the lake. And they launched forth. But as they sailed he fell asleep: and there came down a storm of wind on the lake; and they were filled with water, and were in jeopardy. And they came to him, and awoke him, saying, Master, master, we perish. Then he arose, and rebuked the wind and the raging of the water: and they ceased, and there was a calm. And he said unto them, Where is your faith?..." (Luke 8:22-25).

From this portion of scripture we read that Jesus says to His disciples, "Let us go over unto the other side of the lake." This was the Word of the Lord—the Lord had spoken! Shortly after, a storm came down upon the lake to test this very word spoken to the disciples. They woke Jesus up from resting and sleeping in the lower part of the boat because they were afraid and troubled about the storm. Jesus woke up and rebuked the wind and raging sea, and then He said to His disciples, "Where is your faith?" His inquiry seems to indicate that He expected them to command the sea to be still and the wind to cooperate. This storm exposed the disciples' faithlessness. The storms that are approaching our faith, our families and our nation will expose the essence of our true make up.

The people and the church community of North Carolina were faced with a test and trying of faith. In May 2012, our state went to the poles to vote on a State Constitutional Amendment to affirm the definition of marriage, a point I shared earlier. The amendment defined marriage between one man and one woman as the only legally recognized marriage in the state. The amendment overwhelmingly passed. However, what it also did was expose the hearts and minds of many of the state's citizens. The Bible itself makes it so very clear that marriage can only be between a man and a woman. Marriage was and is God's idea and not man's. I was awed by how many churches and church leaders did not support the amendment. A number of them were very vocal and adamantly against the amendment. Some of those who were sternly against it, said that the amendment was unloving, intolerant and hateful. Of the one hundred counties in North Carolina seven counties did not have a majority of votes for the amendment to pass. I was surprised by those stats. Mecklenburg County, where I reside, was one of those seven counties. It was the trying and testing of our faith and

I believe Mecklenburg County and six other counties failed their test. What was also very revealing is that Charlotte (a city in Mecklenburg County) is reported to have more churches per capita than any city in the entire world. Yes, I said the entire world! Yet, it did not have enough clarity of God's will to affirm the definition of marriage.

There will continue to be storm winds confronting our faith and commitment to God's will and His Word. America and the American Church is facing mounting storm winds that will weigh and prove our commitment to morality and justice; and most of all a storm that will test and try our faith towards the God who made it great. Nations, churches and individuals are often faced with the test of proving and examining the genuineness of their faith. The nation of Israel was faced with such a time, and its leader Joshua affirmed that he was committed to live and serve the one true Living God.

> *"But if serving the Lord seems undesirable to you, then choose for yourselves this day whom you will serve, whether the gods your ancestors served beyond the Euphrates, or the gods of the Amorites, in whose land you are living. But as*

for me and my household, we will serve the Lord" (Joshua 24:15) (NIV).

Wisdom to Remember: As we believe so shall we receive, consequently the quality of our lives is in direct proportion to the measure of our faith in God!

Chapter Ten

FINAL CHARGE

"If My people who are called by My name will humble themselves, and pray and seek My face, and turn from their wicked ways, then I will hear from heaven, and will forgive their sin and heal their land."
(Second Chronicles 7:14) (NKJV)

To you, my fellow servants in <u>Fivefold Ministry Leadership</u>, I charge you to hold fast to the Infallible Written Word of God. We are witnessing the ongoing assault upon the inerrancy of Holy Scripture. The enemy of our soul has consistently come against the truth of God's Holy Word. As the enemy said in the Garden of Eden, "Hath God said?" His evil assault is to bring doubt and question to Holy Scripture. As the Apostle Paul instructs young Timothy, we too need to be reminded of the hour in which we live.

"Preach the Word! Be ready in season and out of season. Convince, rebuke, exhort, with all

longsuffering and teaching. For the time will come when they will not endure sound doctrine, but according to their own desires, because they have itching ears, they will heap up for themselves teachers;" (Second Timothy 4:2,3) (NKJV).

To those who are honored to Pastor and Shepherd God's church, I encourage you to live what you preach. Give yourself to the ministry that you have been graced to serve. Lead, feed and care for God's church as the Holy Spirit instructs and directs. The Lord had some very choice words for those shepherds of Israel who took advantage of His flock for their own selfish gain.

"Therefore, you shepherds, hear the word of the Lord: 'As I live,' says the Lord God, 'surely because My flock became a prey, and My flock became food for every beast of the field, because there was no shepherd, nor did My shepherds search for My flock, but the shepherds fed themselves and did not feed My flock' — therefore, O shepherds, hear the word of the Lord! Thus says the Lord God: 'Behold, I am against the shepherds, and I will require My flock at their hand; I will cause them to cease

feeding the sheep, and the shepherds shall feed themselves no more; for I will deliver My flock from their mouths, that they may no longer be food for them'" (Ezekiel 34:7-10) (NKJV).

The church belongs to the Lord Jesus Christ and we must not use them for our own personal gain. The Fivefold ministers are a gift from God to His church, may we live and lead as just that—a gift from God.

I am hearing consistently within my soul, "Prepare!" Far too many members in the American Church are totally unprepared for the events and opportunities that are before us. Yes, opportunities are before us! The church of this hour has an opportunity unlike any previous time to proclaim the eternal truth of Jesus Christ. The technology of global communications has opened doors that have never been available before. I would also like to encourage those of you who are in other forms of Church Leadership to prepare your congregations for whatever we may face as a nation and as the church of the Living God. The church is the salt of the earth and the light of the world. But, just how prepared are we in preserving lives and reflecting God's eternal light? As the earth quickly advances to the Coming of Jesus Christ (Rapture), just how prepared is the average congregation in caring for lost, unsaved, hurting people? Yes, we do serve by the power of the Holy Spirit. Yet, there are a number of things He has charged us to do. Pastors, leaders and friends please train and equip your congregation to effectively share the Gospel of Jesus Christ. Prepare and educate your people to love and care for the displaced masses no matter their ethnicity, creed, gender, or nationality. I so believe that the hour is upon us and the hurting world will once again look to the church of the Lord Jesus Christ for hope, direction and salvation. Will you and your congregation be prepared to respond?

To the <u>Body of Jesus Christ</u> globally, I charge you to hold fast to the profession of your faith in Jesus Christ. Refuse to give up and refuse to faint in this hour. As Jesus instructed the 1st century church with the "Great Commission," He also instructs us.

> *"And Jesus came and spoke to them, saying, 'All authority has been given to Me in heaven and on earth. Go therefore and make disciples of all the nations, baptizing them in the name of the Father and of the Son and of the Holy Spirit, teaching them to observe all things that I have commanded you; and lo, I am with you always,*

even to the end of the age.' Amen" (Matthew 28:18-20) (NKJV).

My dear brothers and sisters we have an eternal work to do. We are to do the work of an Evangelist in order that men and women, young and old, would be reconciled to God. Distressed and broken lives await our obedience of bringing the Gospel of Jesus Christ to them. The good news of Jesus Christ is the only true hope this world has. The Gospel of Jesus Christ is the power of God unto salvation for everyone who would believe. In this gospel, the righteousness of God is revealed from faith to faith.

I beg of you children of the Most High to know and to rehearse this essential truth:

> *"...you are a chosen generation, a royal priesthood, a holy nation, His own special people, that you may proclaim the praises of Him who called you out of darkness into His marvelous light"* (First Peter 2:9) (NKJV).

Because we are God's own people, for His own glory and good pleasure, let us live set apart unto Him.

> *"Therefore 'come out from among them and be separate, says the Lord. Do not touch what is unclean, And I will receive you. I will be a*

Father to you, And you shall be My sons and daughters,' Says the Lord Almighty" (Second Corinthians 6:17,18) (NKJV).

To live set apart unto Jesus Christ does not mean we have no care, concern or compassion for the lost world around us, but what it does mean is that we refuse to become entangled with meager temporal cares of this evil world system.

Be assured that you are ordained to live a victorious life in Jesus Christ. You are an over-comer in life through the finished work of Christ Jesus your King. The Lord greatly compensates those of us who overcome. He declared that when He comes His rewards are with Him, to give to everyone according to their works. Glory to the Most High God!

Believe God for great and awesome things. Remove the limits off of your faith in God and reach unto Him for your highest expectations. Yes, even in turbulent, troublesome times let's believe our Father for His very best. May His will be done on earth even as it is being done in heaven. Refuse to let the storm winds of difficulty cause you to stop believing God for great and mighty things. Believe God for mighty things for your family, community and church. Jesus tells a father whose son was possessed with a devil:

115

"...If you can believe, all things are possible to him who believes" (Mark 9:23) (NKJV).

Believe the Lord for souls to be saved, hearts to be set free from the enemies grasp, and that Jesus would be glorified in all the earth. I am amazed and awed by the statement, "all things are possible to him who believes!" We know that this belief is directed to the Lord. Our faith is in Him who is able to do exceedingly, abundantly above all we can ask or think.

Rejoice my dear brothers and sisters for our Redemption draws near. I am truly confident that Jesus Christ is coming so very soon. We are to look up when we see all of these things occurring. We must decide to rejoice in the midst of a challenging and misdirected generation. Yes, I believe we can rejoice in the midst of a raging storm. How and why? Because the joy of the Lord is our strength! Strength comes from the Lord as we rejoice in His grace, glory and goodness.

To the <u>un-churched, un-prepared and un-saved,</u> my heart greatly pains for you. Nothing in this life nor in all of eternity is more important than you having a personal relationship with Jesus Christ. There is nothing in this earth more valuable and more precious than your eternal soul. Jesus Himself affirms this as recorded in Matthew 16:26:

"For what profit is it to a man if he gains the whole world, and loses his own soul? Or what will a man give in exchange for his soul?" (NKJV)

Turn over the controls of your life to Christ today and He will give you Himself who is true life. Call upon the Lord Jesus this very day and you will be saved from the eternal judgment of sin and death. I urge and beg of you to ask Jesus Christ to come into your heart this very moment. God the Father loves you and He's not angry with you; He longs for a meaningful eternal relationship with you through His Son Jesus Christ. After accepting God's Son, quickly look for a Bible believing, Bible teaching church. The Holy Spirit will lead you if you ask Him to help you. After finding the church the Lord directs you to, get connected, get involved and get to work.

To all of you true Americans who love this nation, I ask that you pray for the mercy of God to rest upon us. This nation needs an urgent about face. The America that hundreds of thousands willingly give their lives for is at the brink of being no more.

America's three hundred and thirty-eight years of documented existence is in jeopardy. This list of vulnerabilities and sins have been stated and listed above, and apart from divine intervention I believe devastation, disaster and difficulty are sure.

As you pray for God's mercy, seek Him for insight and wisdom for His leading in choosing our elected leadership. America is in desperate need of godly, upright, morally sound, Christ centered leadership to help lead a nation back to righteousness. Our elected officials represent America before the nations and before a holy and righteous God. When we choose unrighteous, morally corrupt leaders to represent us we are positioning ourselves, communities and nation for sure judgment. We must cease from electing morally bankrupt and spiritually detached leaders into public office. The Bible advises us in Proverbs 29:2:

> *"When the righteous are in authority, the people rejoice; But when a wicked man rules, the people groan."* (NKJV)

By God's grace we can see this nation turned around, but it will take a people who are willing to seek the heart and mind of a benevolent God. We must call upon the Lord who made this nation great, to lead us back to Himself!

America must also return to priority living by putting first things first. We must return to our spiritual roots, the Bible! After we affirm our relationship with the God of the Bible we must return to our families. Marriage must once again be esteemed as central to our family's stability. I believe that as America returns to the God who made it great and we return to the family that once sought Him, then His grace will once again rest upon our land. A very popular and fitting Bible verse being voiced by many today is Second Chronicles 7:14:

> *"if My people who are called by My name will humble themselves, and pray and seek My face, and turn from their wicked ways, then I will hear from heaven, and will forgive their sin and heal their land"* (NKJV)

Oh, how we desperately need God's grace to heal our land. Will you petition the heart and mercy of God for His grace to remain upon America? Will you do your part by following the counsel stated in Second Chronicles 7:14? I urgently call upon you to join the countless others who love this nation and are willing to seek and call upon Almighty God for America's preservation.

Is there still hope for America? What will it take in order for the United States of America to avert the approaching storms of adversity? I envision America in a similar state as the famed ship "Titanic." They were heading towards a horrific calamity while most of the passengers and crew had no clue of what lay before them. Most Americans are totally oblivious to and/or deceived about the true state of our nation. There are a host of hidden dangers lingering beneath the waters before us, and countless recognizable hazards as well. The dangers are real and urgent action is needed now!

There is a short season of hope for our nation, and that hope rest in the bountiful mercy of the God who sits and watches over the nations. America's only hope rest in Christ alone, for He is a longsuffering and merciful God. Yet, we also know that He is equally righteous and just. Let me make this so very clear! I believe that the Lord has revealed to me and numerous others that America is poised for unprecedented judgment and difficulty. It will be a season of troublesome and perilous times. What must we do? I believe we can learn much from the people of

Nineveh. We shared the events earlier of Nineveh's sins and wickedness which postured them for judgment, but their repentance positioned them for God's mercy. The Prophet Jonah was instructed by God to cry against Nineveh because their wickedness had come before Him. Jonah flees from the call and responsibility of warning Nineveh, but God confronts his senseless rebellion. After three days and three nights in the belly of a great fish Jonah obeys and arrives in the city of Nineveh with God's declared message.

> *"And Jonah began to enter into the city a day's journey, and he cried, and said, Yet forty days, and Nineveh shall be overthrown"* (Jonah 3:4).

Jonah declared that destruction and overthrow was upon them in a matter of days.

> *"So the people of Nineveh believed God, proclaimed a fast, and put on sackcloth, from the greatest to the least of them. Then word came to the king of Nineveh; and he arose from his throne and laid aside his robe, covered himself with sackcloth and sat in ashes...Then God saw their works, that they turned from their evil way; and God relented from the disaster that He had said*

He would bring upon them, and He did not do it" (Jonah 3:5,6,10) (NKJV).

Notice that the people and the nation's leadership all repented and sought the true and Living God. They believed God, repented, turned from their evil ways, and God showed tremendous compassion and mercy upon them.

Just as the people of Nineveh believed God, repented and turned from their wicked ways so must America do likewise! There must be an urgent proclamation to this nation to repent and turn back to the true and Living God. There must also be a significant number and substantial percentage of this nation that will believe God, repent and return to Him before there can be a relenting of the pending disaster. We read of the mercy of God in how He was willing to bestow pity on the twin cities of Sodom and Gomorrah recorded in Genesis 18:16-33. The Lord said to Abraham that He was going to destroy them because there was an outcry against them. Abraham sought the Lord for leniency upon them for the sake of the righteous. The Lord said He would spare them for the sake of fifty righteous, then forty-five, and even unto ten righteous. What a loving and compassionate God we serve. As we seek the heart and face of the only true God we must remember that He has no delight in the death of the wicked and He is not willing that any would perish, but that all would come unto repentance.

Wisdom to Remember: The eternal rewards and blessings of heaven far exceed the temporal pains and pitfalls of this present life. Therefore, refuse to give up, to give in, or to give out.

CONCLUDING REMARKS

I am hearing over and over in my heart, "prepare" for the opportunities and challenges that lay before the nations — opportunities for those who are devoted to living for the Lord and the proclamation of the good news of Jesus Christ, and challenges for all who's hope is in anything or anyone other than Him.

Watch and pray! We must be a people and a nation that are watching for the appearing of our Risen King. Watch by taking the time to search the scriptures to know the hour and season in which we live. As we watch may we also earnestly pray for God's mercy and grace to remain upon America and the nations of the world. Not only watch and pray, but also prepare. Prepare your own heart to be faithfully living a set apart life unto Christ Jesus, according to God's Holy Word. Our Father is a longsuffering and loving God, who finds no pleasure in the death of the wicked. Let's return to seasons of passionate and purposeful prayer. There must be a people who will seek the Lord with their whole hearts, petitioning the Father for open doors to effectively proclaim the Gospel of Jesus Christ, knowing that the Gospel of Jesus Christ is the power of God unto salvation to all who believe!

America, as well as all the nations of the world, seriously need a great awakening to the truth of the good news of Jesus Christ. He alone is the hope for the nations.

Repent for the King is at hand. The people of God must lead the way in genuine heartbroken repentance. There must be a sincere repentance that brings about personal, recognizable change to a people and to a nation. This authentic repentance should reignite our love and obedience to God and a loving regard for one another. A bona fide repentance turns from all known sin and returns to the God of the Bible. The axe of judgment is laid at the root of the tree, therefore we can no longer pick and choose what sins we will or will not turn from. Repent for the King is at hand!

Prepare for the uncertain events that are before us. I have laid out a number of critically important steps that are necessary to be prepared for the pending changes. Please do not ignore the counsel and warnings to put all of your affairs into proper order. Now is the hour to make ready and be prepared.

The Prophet Ezekiel was given a word from the Lord about the importance of the watchman who cries out and warns his generation of pending danger. Every generation needs watchful intercessors that can discern and see the storm clouds forming, and then boldly sound the alarm so that lives and nations will be spared the approaching danger. We who are born of God must cry out to our generation that many might hear, repent and turn to the Living God. If we fail to warn this generation, then their blood will be upon our hands.

> *"Son of man, speak to the children of your people, and say to them: 'When I bring the sword upon a land, and the people of the land take a man from their territory and make him their watchman, when he sees the sword coming upon the land, if he blows the trumpet and warns the people, then whoever hears the sound of the trumpet and does not take warning, if the sword comes and takes him away, his blood shall be on his own head. He heard the sound of the trumpet, but did not take warning; his blood shall be upon himself. But he who takes warning will save his life. But if the watchman sees the sword coming and does not blow the trumpet, and the people are not warned, and the sword comes and takes any person from among them, he is taken away in his iniquity; but his blood I will require at the watchman's hand'"* (Ezekiel 33:2-6) (NKJV).

There is a storm coming and a merciful warning cry has gone out. The warning sound of the watchman's trumpet is sounded and declared in the land! Who will hear, who will take heed, who will respond to the warning, and who will prepare and make ready? **"Storm Warnings"**

Endnotes

[1] Kenneth Copeland, "What About 2012?" *Kenneth Copeland Ministries*, November 10, 2011 <http://www.kcm.org/real-help/prophecy/what-about-2012>

[2] Pastor Christopher Cookhorne, Bethel Worship Center, Charlotte, NC

[3] Dr. Bill Hamon, *Christian International Ministries* <https://www.christianinternational.com>

[4] Kim Clement, "Prophetic Image Expressions." *The Official Website of Kim Clement* <http://www.kimclement.com>

[5] Dr. Pat Robertson, *The Christian Broadcasting Network*, January 3, 2012 <http://www.cbn.com>

[6] W.E. Vine, <u>Vine's Expository Dictionary of Old and New Testament Words</u>, (Fleming H. Revell Company, 1981) pp. 169-70.

[7] Vine, <u>Vine's Expository Dictionary</u>, pp. 132-3.

[8] Dr. James Strong, <u>Strong's Exhaustive Concordance of the Bible</u>, (Abingdon Press, 1980) Hebrews p. 24

[9] William J. Federer, <u>America's God and Country: Encyclopedia of Quotations</u>, (Amerisearch, 2000) p. 652.